VALUE PROPOSITION

Positioning for Success

Deborah Mills-Scofield

TABLE OF CONTENTS

Chapter 1 Use Market Research to Validate Unconventional Value Propositions
Chapter 2 Develop Value Propositions for Your Customers
Chapter 3 Keep Your Value Propositions Relevant
Chapter 4 Understand Your Users' Pains
Chapter 5 Identify and Prioritize Pain
Chapter 6 Pains and Gains May Change
Chapter 7 Relieve and Eliminate Pains
Chapter 8 Create Category Leaders
Chapter 9 Build a Culture of Constant Experimentation
Chapter 10 Iteratively Test and Evolve Your Business
Chapter 11 Develop Effective Hypotheses for Your Business
Chapter 12 Run A/B Testing
Chapter 13 Expert Insight of Nonprofit
Chapter 14 Strategize with Prenatal and Post-Mortem
Chapter 15 Test for Desirability
Chapter 16 Avoid Confirmation Bias
Chapter 17 Refine Your Target Market
Chapter 18 Climate Industry Expert Insight
Chapter 19 Sustainability Industry Expert Insight
Chapter 20 Eliminate Childhood Hunger
Chapter 21 Build a Hypothesis-Driven Culture
Conclusion
Recommended Resources

CHAPTER 1 USE MARKET RESEARCH TO VALIDATE UNCONVENTIONAL POSITIONING

Have you heard of P&G? They've done an excellent job of creating compelling value propositions over their almost 200-year-long history. One of their most well-known products for the last 77 years, Tide, reached its peak in the late 1990s. They have always been industry leaders. Even if you use products from other brands for your laundry, you definitely know Tide. Many of you have probably compared Tide to other laundry products when deciding what to buy. That's part of the definition of market leadership—when your product is the standard by which other products are judged.

Since Tide has been in the market for decades, P&G has experienced many shifts and transitions in the market and consumers. How do they master their product market fit strategy to continually stay on top? By constantly trying to understand real customers' real needs from multiple angles with multiple market research methods.

P&G Gathered Insights With Focus Groups.

For decades, P&G used focus groups as a key method for market research. They'd get their customers together and ask about a specific product, category, or customer need. In the 2000s, when they were doing a focus group on Tide, P&G learned that people wanted to wash clothes in cold water to save energy and money. Voila, in 2005, when they got the formula right, P&G launched Cold Water Tide, which was a big success.

By directly observing customers, the focus group inspired P&G to find out more details about customers. Instead of just listening to what the customers had to say, P&G's CEO made a controversial decision to have their team directly observe people doing laundry. Why was it controversial? Because, at the time, many of the team members thought it was a total waste of time. They wanted to spend their time on product development and not watch people doing laundry. That bet on observing customers paid off in a big way. The team uncovered a tiny detail that became a pivotal turning point in their product market fit strategy, which led to a big jump in Tide's sales.

A tiny detail was critical to shifting P&G's strategy. When these P&Gers delved deeper into the daily routines of their customers, they saw that putting the cap back on the bottle made a huge mess for customers. This problem was so trivial that the focus group didn't even mention it. That's why it's so important to test from different angles using different testing methods. It's hard to predict whether customer observation will yield better results than focus groups. Isn't it fascinating to see how a simple observation can drastically strengthen a product's value proposition?

P&G didn't just settle for being the best in the industry. They could have easily continued improving the scent or formula of their products, but instead, they took a different approach. By observing and listening to their users, they were able to shift their focus to the user experience. And it certainly paid off. Once they observed the soapy, dripping mess, they discovered a problem that users hadn't truly realized they had. By finding users' problems before the users and competitors, they were able to stay ahead of the game. But here's the thing - users will pick and choose what problem is worse for them then, and they may not even be able to tell you which one they want solved. It's up to you to get out there, observe, and find the real problems that need solving. Because when you do, you'll avoid the risk of disruption.

Did P&G's approach pay off? You bet! They redesigned the bottle and patented the cap, and Tide was flying off the shelves. However, their patent only protected the innovation for a limited time before their competitors found ways around it. Even though P&G remained popular with customers, the value proposition didn't do enough to retain all their customers. When people were presented with other options, they were more likely to choose cheaper brands, just as we saw happen during COVID and the rise of inflation. As a result, P&G's product-market fit shifted as they needed to find other compelling add-on value beyond their initial innovation. You should always be looking for ways to improve your value proposition.

Many other companies have conducted this type of bottoms-up market research. Did you know that Starbucks uses ethnographic research to understand customers' behaviors and desires? They are not just observing how customers order, but what they are doing before and after they order. This approach led to the development of Starbucks' Mobile Order & Pay feature, which allows customers to grab their coffee and go.

Have you ever thought about the products you use in your everyday life and how they solve problems for you? It's easy to take them for granted when they're integrated into your daily existence. If you take a closer look, you'll see that successful products all have a unique value proposition. Besides Tide, P&G has created many successful brands, such as Olay. By observing and addressing their users' pain points, P&G has continued to deliver compelling value propositions to its customers.

What Is A Value Proposition?

A value proposition is the fundamental benefit your product or service provides customers that sets it apart from others and convinces them to choose your product. It is the answer to "why" customers should choose you instead of the competition. Sometimes, your key competitors are more subtle, like "doing nothing" or settling for "good enough."

Therefore, it is critical to validate and continually evolve your value proposition. What do you offer that gives customers value, meaning, and worth? Do you save them time, money, and effort? Do you provide convenience, help them stay safe, or make them feel important? Do you do it well enough for them to pay for that value?

Without a value proposition that provides compelling value to your customers, your product, service, or business won't last long. Consider some products, services, or companies that have disappeared and why they failed.

How Can You Create New Customer Demand?

Coffee is a daily staple for many people, but have you ever thought about how the coffee industry evolved to become what it is today? Let's take a closer look at one of the biggest players in the game: Nestlé.

During World War II, Nestlé developed a new type of instant coffee called Nescafé. Its convenience and long shelf life made it popular among troops. After the war, the convenience of instant coffee made it a popular choice for households, and it gained widespread adoption.

After training the market to like instant coffee, Nestlé wondered whether they could create another demand. However, since instant coffee didn't taste very good, Nestle was looking for a solution that would provide a better taste with convenience. To achieve this, the Nestlé team began researching ways to improve product quality. In 1975, Nestlé employee Eric Favre noticed a small coffee bar near the Pantheon in Rome that was incredibly popular. This inspired him to design the first Nespresso machine.

Nespresso started with a wrong hypothesis. The first Nespresso machine was large and expensive. Given its size and price, the team believed that the machine would not be affordable for most families, so they decided to target businesses instead. The initial product was positioned to let businesspeople make coffee of the same quality as that found in coffee shops in the office by themselves. However, the market proved this initial hypothesis wrong. During focus groups, Nespresso discovered that businesses were not interested in using the machine.

Rather than giving up, Nespresso looked to target a different market by asking Paul Gaillard, a famous salesperson of luxury brands, for his insight. Gaillard assumed that high-income families would value high-quality coffee, so Nestlé tested this assumption. Nespresso shifted its focus to high-income families, lowered the machine price, and increased the pod price. They also changed their packaging and commercial style to meet their audience's expectations.

Nespresso's new and unique positioning resulted in creating new customer demand for luxury coffee. As Gaillard stated, "I wanted to create the Chanel of coffee and decided to keep it chic and bobo." Additionally, Nespresso established membership programs to build personal relationships with all customers who purchased a pod. These programs provided a new channel for market research and enhanced brand loyalty from repeat customers. By 2005, Nespresso had reached its peak.

Keurig later took over Nespresso's success. In 2012, as several key Nespresso patents from 1992 began to expire, they faced fierce competition from newcomers like Keurig, the company behind K-cups. K-cups were able to capture the market share by providing a more convenient and cost-effective solution for coffee drinkers.

Nespresso's failure to anticipate the market shift and adapt its strategies ultimately led to its decline. Unlike Tide, Nespresso didn't seek alternative sources to refine their product market fit, and they didn't think they would lose market share to the competition.

It is critical to continually refine your value proposition, stay ahead of the competition, and, most importantly, exceed your customers' expectations and needs. Nespresso's initial success was due to its ability to gather direct feedback from real customers and make changes accordingly. However, their failure to anticipate the market shift and adapt their strategies ultimately led to their decline.

What Happens When You Stop Listening To Your Customers?

Keurig made billions with their sleek coffee machines and attempted to apply the same strategy to the home carbonation market. Around the mid-2010s, SodaStream created a quiet machine that let you set the amount of carbonation you wanted, and it was priced at around $80. It was a hit, validating the market for home carbonation. Keurig saw SodaStream's growth and, after spending millions of dollars on R&D, jumped in with KOLD.

Instead of conducting market research, Keurig relied on its previous playbook, the one that beat Nespresso. They over-engineered an expensive, lousy solution. KOLD was priced at $370. The machine was big, loud, and came at a time when soda drinking in the USA dropped to a 30-year low. Keurig failed to learn the lesson that helped them beat Nespresso and ended up pulling a Nespresso themselves. Keurig pulled KOLD from the market less than one year after launch.

No matter how great your product or logo is, if it doesn't solve real problems for your customers in a way that fits into their lives, you won't have a lasting business. That's why it's so important to conduct market research and listen to your customers, even if you've had success in the past. Get out there and discover what your customers need and how they need it, and use that knowledge to create a compelling value proposition that will keep you ahead of the game.

Sharpen Your Strategy

Reflect on the following question and refine your approach to achieving product-market fit.

How can a company ensure that it fully understands its potential customers' needs, contexts, constraints, and desires in order to develop a successful product or service with a compelling value proposition?

CHAPTER 2
DEVELOP VALUE PROPOSITIONS FOR YOUR CUSTOMERS

What is a value proposition? A value proposition is how you fulfill the jobs users want or need by alleviating, and maybe even eliminating, their worst pains in doing those jobs and helping them achieve the most important gains or benefits they would have if they had a perfect solution. One of the key criteria in creating a value proposition is identifying something called "Jobs to be Done," which we'll call just "jobs." A job is a task the user needs to do, a problem that needs to be solved, or a need to be satisfied.

A friend of mine, Alex Osterwalder, created the Value Proposition Design, a powerful resource for creating, testing, and vetting value propositions, in which he lays out the Value Proposition Canvas.

The Value Proposition Canvas maps out how your offering meets the customer's needs. First, you will validate the jobs the customer needs or wants to do, the pains they have getting those jobs done, and the gains they would have if they had a perfect solution. Then, you list the ways you think you can alleviate or perhaps even eliminate the customer's pains, the gains you can create for them, and what your product or service is to deliver upon those.

What Jobs Does Zoom Address?

Collaborate remotely and easily meet with people on video and audio. For every job, there are usually several things that make it hard to do. We call these "pains," and the benefits we would have if we had a terrific solution are called "gains."

What are the pains users have when getting these jobs done?
- The then-current solutions required that everyone have the same hardware and software.
- Current solutions were very expensive and only big companies could afford them.
- Mobile devices weren't included in the solutions.
- Setting up a system was extremely complicated.
- The existing systems lacked integration with other systems people used.
- Connections were unstable and sometimes dropped.

Zoom alleviated these pains by making video and audio conferencing software-defined, not hardware-defined, and making it available on virtually any device running any operating system. Zoom integrated with popular systems and services, and they added collaboration tools like the whiteboard, messaging, and more.

What gains would users with these jobs want if the pains of the jobs could be solved?
- They would be more productive because they could reach out to colleagues anywhere and at any time to chat, collaborate, and work together.
- They would save money and time by not having to travel for meetings that could now be done virtually.
- They could pretty much work from anywhere.

Zoom's offering allows users to achieve these gains! Users could indeed reduce travel expenses, increase productivity, and reduce frustration because Zoom was easy to use and provided the freedom to work from anywhere.

Remember, the value proposition is the compelling solution a company delivers to its users to alleviate the worst pains they have doing a job and create the gains, or benefits, they would like to achieve. It's the solution to pains and gains that is hopefully better than anyone else's, including doing nothing and good enough. Zoom certainly did that.

Customers always come first. If you don't start with a deep understanding of what the customer you want to sell to needs to do, the problems they have getting that done, and the upside they'd gain if they had a perfect solution, you risk making something no one wants or needs. Nail the customer profile, and your odds of success are a lot higher!

A job can be a task the user needs to do, a problem that needs to be solved, or a need to be satisfied. Jobs can be:
1. Functional: things you want to do, accomplish, or act on, such as designing a website, developing an application, diagnosing a disease, analyzing data, increasing revenue, increasing profit, decreasing customer churn, etc. In the business world, especially B2B, think of the things people get rewarded for in their jobs, how they are measured and compensated.
2. Social: help the user look good, knowledgeable, smart, chic, credible, be a thought leader, gain social standing, increase one's network.
3. Emotional/Personal: help the user feel good, happy, confident, secure, and safe (both physically and emotionally), in a decision they've made, an investment of time or money.

From the users' perspective, which is best discovered by talking to users, observing them, and asking them questions:
- What couldn't they live without? How many steps are involved in doing this job?
- What are the contexts in which the user does this? Their actions, goals, may change depending on changes in context and constraints. Why?
- Who do they have to interact with to get the job done, or who

has to influence and recommend as part of the job?
- How are they measured in their performance management, and what is involved in meeting those metrics?
- What gives them a sense of satisfaction or nonsatisfaction in doing these jobs, and what makes them feel like they've accomplished that job? Why?
- How do others perceive their role in their organization? How are they perceived by their friends, social network, family, colleagues, etc., and is that the way they want to be perceived? Why?
- What's their interaction with this job throughout the lifecycle of the job? Do they do everything before, during, and after? Does someone else and how does that influence them? Does that change over time? Why? How?

Ask why repeatedly. When a user tells you their job, ask why or what, or when because their job may be more complex than you think.

Several years ago, a major agricultural chemical company decided that since everyone knew weeds are an issue for farmers, the farmer's job the company could solve would be killing weeds. They created and sold a great weed killer. However, that was not the farmer's job. Their job was to have weeds not affect crop yield. That's a very different job, and the solution may very well not be weed killers, as they can negatively affect the soil and ecosystem. The solution could be other technologies, tools, or machinery that prevent weeds from interfering with crop yields. Remember, make sure you've identified the real job.

Sharpen Your Strategy

Consider the venture you are starting, or if you don't have one, think about your favorite product or service.

Outline the tasks you believe your potential (or existing)

customers need to complete or the tasks your favorite product performs for you.

Be as detailed as possible about these tasks. Identify any sub-tasks within the main tasks and prioritize them if possible.

CHAPTER 3 KEEP YOUR VALUE PROPOSITIONS RELEVANT

Netflix lost 200,000 subscribers in the first quarter of 2022. That was their first loss of subscribers in 10 years. Netflix was the archetype of streaming services.

In 2007, Netflix launched its streaming service as its DVD movie rentals declined. A year later, they gave rental subscribers free unlimited streaming to compete with Apple and Hulu. Two years later, Netflix went on a movie signing spree, including the rights from Sony for Breaking Bad. Netflix was on a roll. They negotiated to have the Netflix button on all sorts of remotes, expanded into other countries, increased deals with content providers, and entered the gaming business.

However, Netflix's value proposition was diluted by fierce market competition. For the first time in 10 years, Netflix lost subscribers in 1Q22. While Netflix lost subscribers in 1Q22, Disney+, HBO Max, and Paramount were growing. At the same time, a slew of free, ad-based streaming services were also growing - Tubi (Fox), Freevee (Amazon), Pluto (Paramount), and the Roku Channel. It seems people were willing to watch ads instead of paying a monthly fee, which sounds like the original TV model.

What happened? It's hard to quantify all the factors, but Netflix says the loss is due to three things:

1. Having to stop services in Russia due to the war in Ukraine.
2. Increasing competition.
3. Account sharing.

As for account sharing, Netflix estimates there are about 100 million non-paying households, resulting in a revenue loss of about $1-$2 billion per year. That said, the percentage of shared vs. paying accounts has remained fairly stable. How is this different?

Regarding competition, the number of streaming services in the USA is around 300, and the average household subscribes to four. COVID-19 delayed the inevitable reckoning of a saturated market. While we were trapped inside, we binged, and now that we're going out again, some are binging less. With inflation, people are rethinking what they spend on since food and gas are more expensive. It's a real storm, so real that Netflix, which had vowed never to support ads, now supports an ad-based subscription tier – just like Hulu, Disney, HBO, and others.

Netflix is not alone. We also have another recent streaming fiasco to learn from, CNN+. CNN spent tons of money on big-name talent to launch CNN+, and it only stayed for two weeks. Instead of disrupting the industry as they did in 1980, they were now copying it. Where was the value? They thought it would be in the star anchors and pundits. They were wrong. Why? They didn't take the time to understand viewers' jobs and didn't test their assumptions well enough. They prematurely announced a 1Q22 launch and wouldn't change the date. They didn't ask what would have to be true for people to spend money to watch the people they had watched for free for years. Yes, viewers loved Anderson Cooper, but would they pay to watch him when they could have it for free before? Then there's just the plain old math that didn't work.

- CNN's revenue was about $1.7 billion per year, and the target CNN+ had was to be 10% of CNN's top line, which is $170 million, and break even in its fourth year after a corporate (CNN) investment of about $1 billion in the CNN+ subscription business.
- A CNN+ subscription was $5.99 per month, so about $72 per year, with a goal of 2.4 million subscribers. However, CNN regularly had only about 773K daily users. Where was the 2 million subscriber number coming from? McKinsey told CNN leadership that their subscribership for CNN+ would be more than two times their daily viewership! There is no evidence this number was ever tested or validated.

In February 2022, CNN's president, Jeff Zucker, was fired for improper behavior by the CEO of Warner Brothers (WarnerMedia), who owned CNN. Still, CNN went ahead with the CNN+ launch on March 29, 2022. On April 8th, Discovery bought WarnerMedia, which CNN knew about beforehand. Were they trying to pull a fast one because they knew Discovery wasn't into CNN+ but thought Discovery executives wouldn't un-launch the service? Nope! On April 21, Discovery announced they were shutting down CNN+ on April 30, having less than 10,000 daily active users after two weeks.

There are several lessons to be learned from CNN+, but a critical one is ensuring you meet real customers' real needs. We will cover how critical it is to test assumptions, jobs, pains, and gains in later chapters.

CNN+'s troubles help put what's happening to Netflix in perspective, and Netflix's troubles may be a leading indicator of the streaming industry as a whole. What other "name-brand" services will lose subscribers from some paid plans? Amazon has AWS, e-commerce, and plenty more besides Amazon Prime Video. Apple has a ton of tech products. Disney has theme parks, theater-released movies, and merchandise. Netflix has streaming, and while it's adding gaming, we don't know how big that will be yet.

If You Were Netflix, What Can You Do?

Let's return to pre-COVID days and consider why people subscribe to Netflix. At a root-cause level, there are two main jobs to be done (JTBD):

1. Watch something from home as easily as possible, whenever I want to watch it and on whatever device I want to watch it on, alone or with friends, in-person or virtually.
2. Cancel anytime (and use the 30-day free trial to get a month for free!)

The first job, watching, actually has several sub-jobs that can be just as important to the user:

- Watch a movie that fits my current mood;
- Search the entire library instead of endlessly scrolling;

- Watch something in the background while I multitask;
- Watch something multiple times;
- Not worry about watching something pirated or illegal;
- Watch 24/7;
- Access Netflix original content;
- Rely on the recommendation algorithm;
- Set up user profiles;
- Share accounts up to a certain amount and with added fees;
- No ads;
- Download shows and movies for offline viewing;
- A kid-safe channel.

What would you do if you were Netflix and knew you would lose subscribers in the future? Let's think about what may have caused the shift for Netflix. What new jobs have emerged with so many other streaming options? Given all the intense competition and inflation, do you think streaming users' jobs have changed? Or have the priorities of those jobs changed?

Take note of the new market trends. Conduct experiments to identify new jobs to be done and ultimately develop a different business model. Revisit core assumptions like not having ads on the platform.

◆ ◆ ◆

Sharpen your Strategy

In a world of diverse streaming options, what new jobs have emerged within the industry? How have these new jobs influenced the landscape of streaming services?

CHAPTER 4 UNDERSTAND YOUR USERS' PAINS

BeReal is a new, hot app for sharing photos of yourself in real life, spur of the moment, with no pre-planning. Founded in 2019 in France, it has raised $30m in just two rounds with investors like Andreessen Horowitz. It isn't monetizing the service yet. BeReal is different from other popular social media apps, like Snapchat and Instagram, in several ways.

First, let's analyze social media jobs:

- Keep up with what friends, celebrities, influencers, and family are doing.
- Show off - what I'm doing, wearing, traveling to, hanging out with, how great I look, how cool I am, etc.
- Be in the know of the latest trends.

What sets BeReal apart and is causing its amazing growth is how BeReal is trying to alleviate or eliminate some of the pains experienced by social media users, such as:

1. Increase in poor self-image/self-confidence resulting in increasing mental health issues of youth, some of which are attributed to using social media because of all the

photo-editing, fake backgrounds, and posting of only great, happy things which leads users to feel inadequate, unworthy, stupid, unglamorous, fat, ugly, etc.
2. Concern about how many likes and shares your posts get, which is tied to the previous point.
3. FOMO (Fear of Missing Out).
4. Constant pressure to post all the time and posting only great, cool, happy things.
5. Constant pressure to always look and see what others are doing.

How does BeReal alleviate and eliminate user pains? Let's go pain by pain from above.

1. Pain Reliever for Pain 1 Poor Self-Image/Self-Confidence: BeReal doesn't allow you to post whenever you want to. It prompts you to post - then and only then. You have two minutes to post once prompted, and if you keep retaking a picture, the app shares how many retakes you took. The two-minute warning doesn't give you much time to brush your hair, fancy up, get the perfect lighting, an ideal background, etc. BeReal uses the phone's front and rear cameras to show your real context - the sink with a toothbrush, a bunch of pretzels you're snacking on while studying, whatever you're doing. You can't add filters or edit. This means that you see your friends disheveled, barely awake, running errands, sweaty from working out - in real circumstances, looking like they normally do, so users don't feel like they have to look perfect, glamorous, sexy, toned, perfectly shaped, etc. And that's how your friends

see you too!
2. Pain Reliever for Pain 2 Number of Likes/Shares: BeReal lets your friends react to your posts, but it's not a race to the number of likes and shares, and you can limit your account to just friends, not the public.
3. Pain Reliever for Pains 3-5 FOMO, Constant Post/Read Pressure: Since BeReal doesn't let you post whenever you want to, and it tells you when you're going to post within a quick timeframe, you won't be missing out on anything because everyone is posting at the same time. It's not like everyone will post during the day, and you'll miss it. This also means you are not pressured to post constantly. And that means you are not pressured always to look and see what others are doing. BeReal can feel more like something you do with friends together than other social media.

BeReal makes sharing easy, simple, fast, and authentic. You save time and stress by not having to keep editing your photo to look perfect and worrying if it does. That's a big value proposition because we know the toll social media takes on our youth - BeReal's target market. Their growth is significant - 30% in a month, from 6 million Daily Active Users (DAU) at the end of June 2022 to 7.9 million DAUs at the end of July 2022. If BeReal keeps growing at 30% a month, it will have reached 100 million DAUs in 9 months, which is its stated goal. They are not making money and don't have a business model for making money that's been stated publicly. We know from history that making money with social apps isn't what investors care about - it's the growth and assumption that the service will figure out how to make money.

All this means that it's still too early to tell.

Here, I need to raise an issue around the word 'authenticity.' In the commercial and business world, the concept of authenticity has been created by brands. Brands use authenticity as a value proposition so that you'll buy from them. That doesn't mean they are necessarily inauthentic, but it should give one pause. Gen-Z, BeReal's target market, has never lived without social media and the concept of 'authenticity.' They don't know what it is not to have to perform and appear cool, popular, erudite, whatever the desired impression du jour. Since Gen-Z's birth, parents, teachers, and society have sold them on "authenticity" in a manufactured sense. That makes me wonder if BeReal isn't Deja Vu, a variation on a social media theme instead of something different. What if BeReal is selling the theme of authenticity but not really doing it? Critique the validity of a company's pain relievers, something you should always do. Are you relieving the pain? Are you creating a new pain in the process?

BeReal's success is yet to be determined. They need to discover users' real issues and needs beyond the obvious. A critical aspect is thinking through their pain relievers' second and third-order consequences. For instance, I bet the perception of shaming was not intended, but it's happening. What can BeReal do about it? What about Memories? Is that making people more addicted to BeReal with Streak? It's key to what the users want and how the solutions can positively or negatively impact their lives.

Sharpen Your Strategy

If you are developing a venture, what are the pains you are addressing for your users? Can you prioritize the pains based on your learnings from potential customers?

CHAPTER 5 IDENTIFY AND PRIORITIZE PAIN

How do you get to the root of pain points instead of just addressing the symptoms? Ask "why" several times. Pain points generally fall into three categories:

1. Undesirable outcomes, problems, and characteristics: "X" doesn't work well. It's frustrating. It's not enjoyable.
2. Obstacles: I couldn't do the job well or quickly. It takes too much time or money. It requires too many people.
3. Risks: It'll harm my reputation. We'll get hacked. We'll lose data.

Here are some questions to help you identify your users' pain points:

Financial Questions: These questions revolve around how much something costs, the terms and conditions of payment, and pricing. Ask questions like:

1. Is it too expensive? And if it's too expensive, how do they define expensive? Is it just money, and how much is too much? Is it time or effort, and if so, how much is too much time? 10 minutes, 30 minutes? Why?
2. Is the length of a product or service's life reasonable?

This question is how long the product/service will last before it has to be replaced, repaired, resubscribed to, or thrown out and bought again. Sometimes, users buy something less expensive because it's cheaper. Then it breaks down more often, and they must buy a new one.
3. What else do they have to pay for? There can be associated expenses, such as a payment plan versus a one-time payment, increased subscription fees, and service fees.
4. Is the pricing confusing? There can be unit pricing confusion. Sometimes, buying in bulk saves time and money. Additionally, disposable items are usually more expensive, but they are more convenient time-wise.
5. What are the overall product lifecycle costs? These include maintenance costs, keeping the product in good shape, and updating or upgrading as required. For example, getting a car serviced regularly.

Functional Questions: These revolve around actually using the thing.

1. What gives them a headache when trying to do this job? What frustrates them? Why?
2. What's underperforming? What's missing? Are there annoying features? Malfunctions? Is it too easy to set up incorrectly or make mistakes? Why?
3. What things or parts of the job are hard to do or create a lot of resistance? Why?

Social/Emotional Questions: These get to how they feel when they use the "thing." Do they worry? Are they thrilled? Are they worried about their reputation?

1. What keeps them up at night? Why?
2. What tends to go wrong or is very annoying? Why?
3. What keeps them from having a great solution? Cost? Difficulty in learning? Other obstacles? Why?

To put learning the importance of asking these questions to uncover pains in a concrete example, let's use Uber. Did you know Uber started in March 2009, during the financial crisis, when the founders couldn't find a taxi in Paris? Try finding a cab in NYC in the '80s through Aughts, especially when it rained. From the individual user's perspective, the jobs were 1) needing to get somewhere quickly and not having a car or 2) wanting to go carless.

What are the pains of getting these jobs done?

If we look at the types of questions to ask to identify pains, we can match them up a bit with the pains using the Uber example.

1. Financial questions elicit pains about how expensive cabs are, how hard it is to split the fare with others, and how you may need multiple cabs if you have a lot of people.
2. Functional questions elicit pains about the very long waits for a cab, how they never show up in bad weather, how you don't know if they will show up at all or if it's even on its way if you called for one, how disgusting and messy cabs can be, and how hard it is to tell them where exactly you are.
3. Socio-emotional questions can highlight pains similar to functional questions - like the frustration of waiting

for a cab, worrying if it will show up, and staying up at night worrying if the cab you called for will show up for your early morning flight.

Airbnb is another great example of jobs and pains. Let's examine Airbnb from both the hosts' and business travelers' perspectives.

Hosts have three major jobs:

1. Make extra money from the "fixed asset" - unused rooms with grown-up kids or no kids, which has even morphed into a whole Airbnb business of buying real estate for "Airbnbbing."
2. Showcase their area and city.
3. Meet interesting people they wouldn't otherwise meet.

What are the pains of getting these jobs done?

- Safety and security in knowing who is renting from them, especially if they're renting a room in their home while they are there.
- Confidence in getting paid by the renter.
- Liability insurance for hosts and renters, let alone any issues that will leave bad reviews.
- Marketing - getting the word out that you have space to rent.

Business Travelers have four major jobs:

1. Getting a higher value for their money depending on the host's accommodations versus a hotel.
2. Meeting interesting people who are not from work.
3. Getting to know the area better, especially if they will be there often or are considering relocating.

4. Feeling more at home for longer stays.

What are the pains they have getting these jobs done?

- It's hard to find a place to rent - where do you start looking?
- Feeling like you're imposing on someone, even if they offer it.
- Concern about not having the usual hotel amenities.
- Trust that it's a safe place, and you won't get ripped off or hurt.

Airbnb provides a safe, vetted way for hosts and business travelers to get these jobs done.

Let's talk about electric vehicles (EVs). We'll do an after-the-fact 2019 job analysis.

It's August 2019. You're talking to potential buyers about their jobs to be done. They mention the need for personal mobility to run errands, go on vacation, take kids to soccer practice, and commute to work. And they'd like a vehicle that is good for the environment, hence an EV.

Potential buyers had a lot of pains regarding buying an EV. Were EVs as safe as combustion engine cars? How often did you have to charge? How long did it take to charge? Where could you charge because there weren't enough charging stations around? Could you get a charging plug installed at your condo? What do you do if your battery dies and you're on the road? What if it's hot and you want air conditioning? Does that sap the battery a lot faster? And if it's winter and you want heat, what does that affect battery life? If you buy now, are you buying at the height of the price? These are a bunch of genuine pains.

Buyers wanted gains like the ability to seat up to 7 or 8 people like a 'regular' SUV, terrific safety ratings, a very long-lasting battery, a long long-distance range, like up to 400+ miles/charge, and sports car performance. For some buyers, another significant gain was a sleek design that makes heads turn and lots of oohs and aahs from friends. Don't downplay this last gain. Many people value prestige and being cool and trendy.

Tesla has been the market leader, ahead of Prius, Leaf, and many other EVs cheaper than a Tesla, so something else is going on besides just wanting an EV. If you probed on the jobs when you asked about an EV, some would say: well, yes, they wanted an EV, but they also wanted something that conveyed status, wealth, and luxury. Hence, Tesla. The job wasn't just having an EV. It was prestige, status, and luxury. But most potential users wouldn't bring that up on the first round of questions. Remember to ask why, and why not, over and over again.

Are you getting the idea of pains? When you ask questions to identify pains, you must dig deeper. Remember how I said you have to ask why over and over? That's because users don't often think about the root causes of their pains. They are focused on the symptoms since they are easily recognizable. Few of us stop and think through the real reasons for the pains.

◆ ◆ ◆

Sharpen Your Strategy

Think back to your chosen products or services. What specific pains have they alleviated or even eliminated for you? Be specific about why the solution does a great job of addressing the pains. If you're working on a venture, write down the specific pains your users experience today and how you plan to address them.

Then start listing the gains: What amazing gains does this product or service provide? What gains would your users just love? They may not be the ones you're thinking of providing yet.

Remember, some pains are worse than others, so try to prioritize them if you can. Start with High, Medium, and Low. This is important because in creating a compelling value proposition, you don't have to solve all the problems, just the most critical ones. Sometimes, solving one major pain makes the rest less relevant and painful. If the perfect solution fell from heaven, what gains would your users experience?

CHAPTER 6 PAINS AND GAINS MAY CHANGE

Think of a gain as the benefit you get if you have the perfect solution to the job. If a pain is that doing "X" is frustrating, a gain would be that it's easy and intuitive to do, so you get it done fast, and now you have more time to do other things. It could be that existing solutions are costly and limited in functionality, but now there is a simple, inexpensive, feature-rich offering. Those are gains.

A gain is **not** something that works as it should. A gain isn't having your car start in the winter. Yes, the car not starting is a pain, but the car starting is not a gain. It's the normally expected state.

A gain makes doing your job easier, cheaper, more productive, more fun, and maybe even more important. Gains, when done well, can even provide benefits you didn't think you could have. Gains can give you more time to do other things or make you feel special or respected.

We've talked about the users' jobs and pains that Netflix addresses. But what about gains? Why did so many people subscribe to Netflix in the first place? It had to solve some of the pains in getting those jobs done. Here were some big gains Netflix provided:

- Being able to watch shows and movies without the internet
- Having the show stop when you fall asleep with the timer feature

- Previewing the show before watching it
- Watching with friends, no matter where they are, which was a bonus during COVID
- Categorizing content based on interests and similarity
- Recommendations based on your viewing history
- Multiple devices and accounts
- No ads

The Value Brought By Gains To Users Can Change Over Time.

Gains are wonderful until they become expected by the user. What was once a gain often becomes expected over time. This means that if you don't provide that gain, you're not even in the running competitively. Perhaps this is part of Netflix's problem today. Look at the gains above. Hulu, Amazon Prime, Disney+, Paramount+, and others provide these same gains and more.

You may wonder whether gains are just the solved pains. Sometimes they are, but sometimes they're not. You must dig deeper and ask more and better questions to find the difference. For example, say you're going out to lunch, you pay with your credit card, and it doesn't work for some reason. That's a pain. But if it does work, that's not a gain. That's how it should work in the first place. Let's say your morning routine is to stop at Dunkin for your Macchiato with coconut milk and a mocha swirl. You know it usually takes about 7 minutes from order to having your drink in hand. If one day, you get it in 4 or 5 minutes, that's a gain. If another day takes 10 minutes, that's a big pain. And if it's fifteen, you're hopping mad. If the coffee comes lukewarm, that's a pain. And if it's too hot, that's also a pain - you're like Goldilocks. You want it just right. What does this tell us?

Sometimes pains and gains are on an expectations spectrum. Depending on the context and constraints, a pain can be a gain, and a gain can be a pain. It all depends on what, where, when, and how you're doing what you're doing.

The lesson? Gains are not always the opposite of pains. But how do you avoid falling into that 'opposite' trap? By looking at the expectation spectrum and finding where, when, why, and how not meeting the expectation can be a pain and when it could be a gain. When getting your morning coffee, if you're in a hurry, the normal 7-minute wait can become a pain, making a 3-4-minute wait golden! And, if 3 or 4 days in a row it's a 3-4 minute wait, now that's the expectation, and 7 minutes, which was normal, is now a big pain. But if one morning, you start a conversation with someone in line, and you don't realize 10 minutes have passed and you've made a new friend, then the 10-minute wait isn't a pain. Sometimes, there may be a clear, unchanging boundary on the expectations spectrum between pain and gain. In other cases, you may have to probe and dig deeper to spell out the limits and endpoints of the expectations spectrum. Knowing these subtle differences will help with your hypothesis testing and prototyping, which we'll cover later.

Sometimes jobs change, as we saw in the previous chapter on Netflix. Sometimes the job stays the same over time. Many times, pains and gains change, thereby changing potential solutions. As people got used to the gains, the gains became the expected norm, increasing the degree of 'gain-ness' a gain needed to have to be a gain. Gains come in various sizes and shapes. In the eating-out example, having your credit card work vs. not work is not a gain - it's how it should function in the first place. They're working as expected.

Ask these questions to discover the gains:
- What types of savings, in terms of time, money, and effort, would be unexpected, desired, and incredibly valuable to your users?
- What outcomes do users love to have that they wouldn't normally expect or think possible, perhaps around quality, performance, cost, lifetime use, ease of use, more features,

fewer features, more credibility, a great reputation, level of expertise or knowledge? And not just outputs (like more hours) but outcomes (like time to spend with your family).
- What level of performance would delight users - speed, reliability, durability, environmental conditions, features?
- What aspects can make users' lives or work easier, like more or fewer services, the total cost of ownership, usability, accessibility, and more time?
- What could provide your users with more positive social standing - make them look good, chic, 'in-the-know,' credible, authority, or power?
- What specific intangibles would users love, like the amazing sleek design, warranties, and guarantees, personalized services?
- What are the ways to fulfill users' aspirations and hopes, relief from physical/psychological/emotional pain or suffering?
- What are the ways users can adopt a solution faster because it's less expensive, less investment of time/resources/money, less risky, higher quality, great performance, and fabulous design?

Gains may vary and overlap, depending on whether you're B2C and B2B. B2C gains are usually, but not always, about gaining time for you and your loved ones, saving money, improving one's image/prestige, lowering stress, and having a better quality of life. For B2B, gains are usually around ways to help customers save money, make money (raises and bonuses for the individual, revenue, profit, market valuation for the organization), gain market share, enter/create a new market, save/re-allocate time and resources, improve (individual/corporate) reputation, gain/retain followers, attract and retain employees and partners, get investors, etc.

Before we get to the homework, let's go back to a few previous examples and identify the gains. What are the gains for BeReal users through our non-cynical lens? More time (since you're not scrolling to infinity) to do whatever you want (study, spend time with friends, party), less anxiety over FOMO, increased self-esteem because you now know you don't always have to look perfect, and a deeper level of relationships with friends seeing them as they are.

We talked about Zoom earlier, but it is worth repeating. If users had a great solution, they'd save money because they wouldn't have to travel, they'd save time because they're not traveling or commuting, they could use the app on any device and with someone on any devic, intuitively and easily, and they'd be more productive because all the time traveling wouldn't be wasted, and they could work from anywhere. Those are big gains.

Sharpen Your Strategy

Think about your venture's offering or your favorite product or service. Will your offering become the new status quo? What would happen if your offering becomes expected?

List out circumstances where your pain relievers may no longer relieve pains, or your gain creators become pains over time. Explain how you could address them.

CHAPTER 7 RELIEVE AND ELIMINATE PAINS

Kinder Joy is one of the products I wish had been available when my kids were little. It's a candy treat for kids with a toy inside, but there's no mess with the toy. Let's assume that one of Kinder's target customers is moms, especially busy moms.

We'll narrow it down to a few pains that busy moms have:

- Having toys to keep the kids entertained while running errands, usually in the car, doing something else you need to do without being interrupted by kids;
- Kids grumbling that they only get healthy treats;
- And the worst pain: treats that make a huge mess when there's no time to clean up. Treats that have toys in them usually mean the toys are messy from the treat, so the mom has to carry all sorts of wipes to clean the kids and the car, which means more stuff to schlep again.

Kinder Joy solves the above pains wonderfully. It is a plastic egg that pulls apart in half, with each side sealed. One half is the treat - creamy, custardy stuff with wafers and chocolate - and the other is the toy. Kinder Joy solves a real pain: The big pain of giving your kids a treat and toy without making a mess is solved by Kinder Joy.

When you look at customer pains, prioritize them based on what the user thinks is the worst to the least bad. You want to target the worst pains because by relieving those, you can make a huge positive difference for the user.

Going back to the first chapter, remember how Tide relieved two big user pains? They made the formula work in cold water to get clothes as clean and bright as warm and hot water. They redesigned the cap, so there is no more messy soap all over everything. Airbnb's most important pain reliever was assuring trust - vetting hosts and guests to assure safety and security. Tesla relieved the key pains of range, safety, and style. Netflix had done a bang-up job of addressing pains until others did, too. While Netflix had done a great job at relieving key pains, there are now new customer pains they're not addressing well enough to keep them, let alone attract new customers.

As you think about ways to relieve users' worst pains, think about ways you can save them money, time, and frustration. Think about how you can help them feel better and achieve their desired performance. Think about how you can eliminate social risks, financial risks, or technical risks. Think about how you can reduce common user errors and mistakes, lower up-front investment, and flatten the learning curve. Think about how you can eliminate or reduce other obstacles to adoption. Be specific on how you plan to relieve the pain, not cause new ones.

You also need to understand what users do before, during, and after they do the job. Sometimes, by relieving the worst pains, the other pains don't matter as much. Sometimes, the pains go away or ease up or become irrelevant because you relieved the worst ones.

You also need to be aware of interactions between pains. For instance, pain could be that the job is very frustrating and time-consuming. Let's imagine you are putting together a Lego kit for your child or putting furniture together (including all those extra screws that should have gone somewhere). A pain reliever, depending on the job, could be doing this with friends, which makes it **seem** less frustrating and time-consuming. In this case, the gain wasn't based on reducing the level of frustration but adding the 'feature' of doing it with someone you like being with.

There's a subtle and critical aspect to relieving pain: make sure you truly understand the root cause of the pain. If you don't, you can create more pain for the user by trying to solve it.

Let's talk about an app that was created to reduce or eliminate the pain of getting family members to do their fair share of household chores. It's usually the woman who does most of the housework. Apps like Cozi were created to help reduce the pain of doing most of the housework.

The job was household chores - as in, not having to do all the household chores yourself. The most common user is female, married or in a relationship, and most likely with kids. She wants to split the chores with her partner ideally.

The pains? Most male partners in heterosexual relationships don't do their fair share of the chores. Either the woman nags, which we know isn't a good thing, or does them and can become a bit resentful (a big pain for everyone). Another pain is that most partners think of chores as physical chores - laundry, cleaning, trash, food shopping, and cooking. That said, if you're a mom reading this, you know full well that there are a ton of "invisible" chores to do every day - like scheduling hair or medical appointments, organizing sports schedules, extracurricular, rides, planning vacations, making up shopping lists, and shopping. Making many daily decisions to keep the family running also means anticipating everyone's needs.

The ideal gain would be to have your partner and kids help with the chores. Perhaps another wonderful gain could be having you and your partner set a model for your children to see and understand how sharing household responsibilities is for both partners.

Cozi, and several other companies, developed applications to help the main chore-doer coordinate and delegate chores to partners and kids. But what they didn't realize, because they didn't test their assumptions, was that instead of alleviating the pain, like no time and all the effort to do the chores, they added yet another pain.

The new problem they created was huge and became a major flaw in the app. Cozi's solution to use technology to manage everyone doing chores added more work without actually getting any chores done. The app, for the most part, put the burden on the woman to manage chores, even though she was already managing the chores. She wanted others to help with the chores and didn't want to spend her precious time entering things into an app.

How Did This Happen?

In trying to understand customer pain, Cozi did not delve deeply enough to understand the root causes. For example, when users said something was painful, they did not ask why it was painful. Or they did not test the hypothesis that their app would relieve the pain. The app created more work for the user, not less.

One of the best ways to ensure that your pain reliever relieves users' pain and does not create more is to test your hypothesis that your pain reliever will actually relieve pain. We'll delve much more into hypothesis testing in an upcoming chapter, but I want you to start thinking about it now.

Your pain relievers are hypotheses. You will test to discover and validate with iterative prototyping and user feedback. Identify which of your core hypotheses is most critical to the success of your venture. And which ones, if they are false, make or break the business. Test those first.

Sharpen Your Strategy

Think of ways to relieve pains for your venture or how your favorite product has done that for you. Identify the root cause of the pains. Make sure you're not addressing the symptoms.

CHAPTER 8 CREATE CATEGORY LEADERS

Creating the gains that customers want is great. This is one of the hardest things to do. Sometimes, you discover new customers in an existing market. Other times, you create an entirely new market.

Have you heard of Cirque du Soleil, the "circus-theater" company that created a new entertainment genre? How did they do this? By creating a set of gains that disrupted their industry and surpassed customers' gain expectations. The typical job a circus fulfilled for customers was experiencing thrills, fun, and humor at a reasonable price. Circuses had been doing this job for decades. What were the evolving customers' pains and desired gains that Cirque du Soleil saw in a circus?

Customer Pains	Customer Gains
Ticket prices	Value-based prices for what they were getting
Muddy venues, not fun in bad weather	Comfortable, dry venue
Increasing anger of the use & treatment of circus animals	No animals at all
Fun, thrills, humor, and danger for the whole family	Fun, thrills, humor, and danger for the whole family

Cirque du Soleil's response to customers' pains and gains brought things to a whole new level while also reducing Cirque's costs. Animals and star circus performers cost a lot of money. The setup, take down, and maintenance for multiple tents cost a lot of money, too. How did Cirque du Soleil alleviate pains and create gains beyond customers' imaginations? By eliminating the pains and related costs of animals, star performers, and multiple areas, Cirque du Soleil created a unique, refined environment, show themes, and multiple productions with high artistic and choreographic design and music.

Cirque du Soleil created an entirely new entertainment genre. The Cirque du Soleil circus was theater. It is priced similarly to a higher-end circus. Creating an entirely new market is extremely rare. It's not trivial.

Having a remarkable understanding of users and what is possible is the road to success. Think about the iPad. We didn't know we needed iPads before Steve Jobs. He and his team saw an unmet, unarticulated want—not a need—in the market. iPad was yet another elegant, easy-to-use product, which caught on so well that the competition moved in.

What were the user jobs Steve saw? The initial jobs were not heavy-duty computing jobs like number crunching, making presentations, or writing. The initial jobs were emailing, texting, socializing, surfing, reading books, watching videos, looking at pictures, and playing games. As the iPad evolved, more jobs arose as users realized they wanted to do more on the tablet.

Steve Jobs thought a big pain in doing these communication and entertainment 'jobs' was screen size. While you could use an iPhone, the phone screen was small. While you could use your laptop with a bigger screen, it's bulkier and has a lousy battery life. Steve Jobs summed it up as we needed something "more intimate than a laptop, and so much more capable than a smartphone." Voila - the creation of a third type of device - a real tablet.

What was the iPad's value proposition? Size, weight, and big screen... which meant it was very portable. Many people stopped taking their laptops when they traveled and just took their iPads. As Apple added cameras, external keyboards, trackpads, multitasking, and performance levels, it replaced the laptop for a lot of people. Let's compare users' pains and Apple's pain relievers.

Customer Pain	Pain Reliever of iPad
Laptop Weight	5% the weight of an average laptop
Laptop battery life (~ 4hrs)	10-12 hours battery life
iPhone (and other smartphones) have small displays	larger display than smartphones
The complexity of laptops (PC-Windows) and integration with iPhone	Extremely simple with no learning curve if you have an iPhone and easier maintenance
Most laptops are heavy and clunky for travel	very portable with easy connection to the net
	Evolving Pain Relievers with iPad's evolution
Need a laptop to do writing, number crunching, presentations, multitasking	Pages, Numbers, Keynote, Word, Excel, Powerpoint, Adobe Suite, Multitasking added
Regular laptops didn't have good multimedia technology - you either needed a specialized laptop or a desktop that wasn't portable	Great drawing capabilities, recognition and apps for animation, 3D design, AR, handwriting recognition, app store access, music producing, podcast production

What were the gains of the iPad? People would have *loved* a simple, intuitive device that let them do almost everything they could on their laptops—with long battery life, an instant on-and-off switch for travel, and ease of use when putting it on their lap or tucking it under their arm. Dream on. But that's what they got with the iPad! And of course, you could look wicked cool having this thing!

As people got used to the device, they wanted to do more with it, like their creative work. The iPad transformed business and personal computing. I have many clients who bring their iPads to meetings and students who do their artwork and 3D modeling on it.

Remember the expectation spectrum? As people became used to the unique functionality and design of the iPad, they expected and wanted more. That's why you must keep understanding your customers' needs and wants and evolve your product. Many of the iPad's gains were needs or wants users would never have considered. That's the magic of Apple.

Gain creators don't have to be art forms, like Cirque du Soleil, or a product or service, like the Apple iPad. Gain creators can also be experiences, like what Subaru has done with their "Love" campaign.

The Subaru Outback is my favorite car. I live in Maine, which is full of Subarus, probably because they all have AWD (All Wheel Drive) and are fuel-efficient. Subaru did a major rebrand several years ago and is one of the few companies that has consistently used the brand. Have you heard of the Subaru Love Promise? "Subaru and its retailers believe in making the world a better place. This is our promise to show love and respect to our customers and to work to make a positive impact in the world." This unique branding has made Subaru a lifestyle company, not just a car company.

What made Subaru's brand successful? Ever since the power of the Love Campaign, "Love" is expected because this gain has become the norm. Unlike most of corporate America, Subaru has applied the Love campaign throughout its entire company, from creating a culture of Love in how it treats and inspires employees, to how car factories are designed, to how cars are sold and serviced. Such consistency attracts many first-time and repeat buyers who love their cars and the causes.

Now let's focus on the Outback, a classic Subaru. What are the customer gains of the Subaru Outback? Here's a list to get you started:

- **Price/Value:** A well-equipped Subaru lists between $25-36K. To get AWD in other vehicles sold in the USA, you have to buy a premium brand SUV, most of which list for at least $20K more for the same level of equipment as the Subaru, without the fuel efficiency.
- **Impeccable Reputation for safety and quality:** Subarus consistently receive the highest safety ratings because of their superior engineering, technology, and vehicle architecture. They have state-of-the-art crash and injury-reducing technology and are incredible in lousy weather. 96% of 10-year-old Subarus are still on the road.
- **Unique Identity:** They have created a unique identity that is embedded in Subaru's corporate culture from leadership to distribution. It especially shows up in their custom accessory packages and customer service.

How Did Subaru Deliver What Its Customers Want?

Subaru conducted a thorough analysis of their existing and potential customers, not just from a 'why do they buy a Subaru' viewpoint, but from a deep understanding of their customers' lives and passions. Subaru wanted to understand its customers as human beings. Subaru learned that its customers buy experiences, not just products. They are usually well-to-do, educated, financially savvy, and passionate about the outdoors, learning, and exploring, regardless of the weather, and care deeply about their causes.

Subaru focused on the experiences that customers wanted, making them easy to achieve instead of competing with other automakers on typical trends like shininess, glitz, chrome, and muscle-car-like features. This has led to strong customer loyalty for Subaru, resulting in lots of repeat business. Even though Subaru customers tend to be more frugal than the average auto buyer, they still purchase new Subarus. Subaru trains its dealers, mechanics, and service personnel to always show love. That's why "Love is what makes a Subaru, a Subaru." Subaru built its pain relievers and gain creators into the embodiment of a Subaru vehicle and all that surrounds it. The product or service you deliver to the market is just that; the "how" you relieve pains and create gains.

I bet Subaru and its marketing agency did a lot of testing around the key hypotheses driving the "Love" campaign. That testing is critical - we'll discuss more of that in upcoming chapters. To know that what you build will meet the users' needs, you need to test your hypotheses - the things you believe you can do to relieve pains and create gains. Test iteratively so that as you build your product or service, you are getting closer and closer to meeting, and even exceeding, what your users want, need, and expect!

Sharpen Your Strategy

How can you test if the ways you relieve pains and create gains are spot on?

CHAPTER 9
BUILD A CULTURE OF CONSTANT EXPERIMENTATION

Testing is critical in creating a compelling value proposition. Identifying hypotheses and running experiments to validate them never ends. It's the life of a startup. It's the life of a company, no matter what size or stage. And it's never-ending. The day you stop testing is when you better start closing up shop.

Buffer is a values-driven company that provides affordable and intuitive marketing tools for individuals and teams. At its core, Buffer allows users to create and schedule posts to share across many social networks, such as LinkedIn, Facebook, Instagram, Twitter, and Pinterest.

Buffer was co-founded 12 years ago, in 2010, by Joel Gascoigne, who applied lean start-up principles to its development. In 2013, with 10 employees, Joel co-developed Buffer's 10 core values, which they faithfully use to hire and run the company. As of January 2022, Buffer had almost 61K customers and an annual run rate of $18.75M. It raised about $4M and paid back its investors so that it owned all of Buffer and could keep focused on its mission.

Buffer runs by experimentation - constantly prioritizing their evolving key hypotheses, rigorously testing them, and deploying what's been validated. Let's look at a few examples of their hypothesis-testing product development process.

1. In the beginning, Joel Gascoigne, Buffer's founder, started testing the idea of Buffer using a Mock Sale test. In the 2010s, social media users were scheduling posts manually across all the various platforms. Joel thought a scheduling service for social media posts, starting with Twitter, would be valuable to those people. He figured adding a "Plans and Pricing" button on the landing page would be a way to test the need and willingness to pay. When a user clicked, a message would appear saying the service wasn't up yet, but to leave your email to be notified. Joel believed that people would pay a monthly fee to schedule their tweets on Twitter. To test this, Joel put three different pricing plans on the landing page. When a user clicked on one of these options, an email sign-up form appeared saying Buffer was almost ready to launch. The testing results showed the $5/month plan was the most popular. The insight was that people wanted to schedule more than one tweet per day but not an unlimited amount. This was the evidence needed to build Buffer.
2. Buffer repeatedly created an experiment to figure out what to develop next. A few years ago, they ran an experiment to figure out which social accounts Buffer users wanted next. They developed a "Connect" page that, instead of hiding the connections they didn't support at the time (e.g., Facebook Groups or LinkedIn Groups), listed them and let users click on the ones they wanted and explained why they weren't available. These logs gave Buffer great information and gave users a great user experience. First, users got immediate feedback on why the account they wanted to be connected to wasn't available. Second, Buffer collected everyone's emails so that when the connections were available, Buffer

could let those users know. They learned users wanted Facebook Groups from the data. When they notified the interested users that the feature was available, their email got an open rate of 70% and a click-through rate of 18.7%. Not too shabby.
3. Buffer's top priority is to deliver great products and exquisite support to free and paying users. Free has always been important to Buffer. They decided to simplify the free plan to make it streamlined, easier to use, and more valuable. But, before making changes, they did a lot of research into user behavior, asking for constant feedback. The goal was to support as many social media workflows as possible. A critical part of the experiment was getting continual user feedback on changes and being open to being wrong! Buffer started testing some of these hypotheses by simplifying the Free plan user flow.

User feedback was clear - the new changes made the UI/UX more complicated, not less. Some might view this as a failure, that Buffer made things worse for their customers, but because of how they tested these changes and constantly sought user feedback, it wasn't. It was a huge learning experience.

Buffer could have dramatically reduced the functionality of the Free plan, but they didn't. Active Free users are an important part of Buffer and its culture, making social media management easier so people can share more. The more users, the larger their sample size to test new options, features, and services.

Buffer continues to share how it evolves its services and runs the company on its "Open" blog. It creates a lot of trust, loyalty, and community-building. Buffer users know they can influence the product and have an impact. That goes a long way toward increasing customer acquisition and retention.

Netflix and Buffer are in different industries with different types of customers, and the responses to their changing markets are very different. Their main difference lies in culture. Netflix published its famous culture deck in 2009. They were the definition of a great culture startup. Buffer also focused on culture from the outset, which is rare in the startup world. Buffer has been thoughtful about its culture. Check out Joel's 10-year reflection and Buffer's ten core values. What is the difference?

Both have great cultures, but their cultures have an underlying philosophical difference. Buffer's culture is one of reflection, speed and values. Many people think being reflective means you're slow to respond, leading to paralysis by analysis. But in Buffer's case, it's an AND, not OR, because their constant testing means they can be data-driven and make informed, reflective decisions quickly. By running experiments, they learn and apply what's validated. They don't feel that everything has to be deployed tomorrow. A feature or a product can be launched a week or even a bit more after validation if more reflection is needed. This doesn't mean they don't take risks. They take calculated risks.

The company is run like one big experiment - with the open-mindedness and willingness to change what they offer and how they are structured to offer it. This includes how they hire, onboard, reward, and operate. Buffer has a culture of humility - it's about their users and their employees, not them. Buffer has turned down acquisition offers and bought out their VCs to give themselves the freedom to live their values and meet the evolving needs of their users.

As for Netflix, I don't know how well they have retained and grown their culture, but it seems they have lost touch with what their users want. Do they know what unique jobs their users have today? Not six months ago, not at the beginning of COVID, but now? Do they have hypotheses to test how they can relieve users' pains and create gains? Do they even know what these are today? Do they realize they are increasingly competing with 'good enough'?

A company's success always comes down to its leadership.

Leadership shapes key decisions and sets the company culture. Leadership with a sense of hubris loses touch with the customers and people who helped them grow. Stay humble. It's never about you.

◆ ◆ ◆

Sharpen Your Strategy

Consider the culture of your company, whether it's the one you currently work for or the one you're creating. What core values will you hold as sacrosanct? What type of behavior do you want to encourage, reward, hire for, or fire for?

CHAPTER 10
ITERATIVELY TEST AND EVOLVE YOUR BUSINESS

Now that you have identified your value proposition, you need to create a plan to test and assess whether you have nailed product-market fit. To assess product-market fit, we will learn from a company built around iterative experiments and data-driven design: Duolingo.

Duolingo started in 2009 as a research project. To get meaningful data, Luis needed to get Duolingo in front of as many people as possible, which meant making it free. He onboarded thousands of users - a statistically valid sample size for his research - and used the data to apply what they learned.

Initially, Duolingo went after the $300M business translation market. They were a social venture that crowdsources translation work from their free users. In 2011, they raised a $3.3M Series A from Union Square Ventures and Ashton Kutcher before they built any product. The pitch? "Building a sustainable way to generate human translations of the web on a large scale." Then, Luis did a nerdy TED talk and got 300K beta users signed up. One-third, 100K, actually used Duolingo, with more than 500K on the waitlist (which validated the market opportunity). From 2011 to 2012, Duolingo continued to improve. They added more languages and gamified the user experience. They reached 250K active users without implementing any monetization.

How did Duolingo begin to make money? Duolingo's first monetization strategy was offering translation services to media companies. They also planned a B2B self-service translation portal and continued growing usage to strengthen translation services. Customer retention increased significantly, with over 100K users completing a Duolingo course! However, to grow and monetize the B2B market, they need to focus less on the users and more on the businesses.

While B2B had a lot of potential, Duolingo was concerned that serving businesses would distract them from serving their users, which is the foundation of Duolingo. However, if they didn't want to serve businesses, they had to change their business model. To focus solely on users and still monetize Duolingo, they decided to compromise their "never do ads" philosophy and did ads while creating an optional paid plan.

In 2014, they stopped working with all businesses and did something very innovative. They created a new user service called Test Center. They not only changed how they made money, but they also added a new way to make money with Test Center while focusing on serving their users.

Test Center was a major business model upgrade. For many English-language learners, getting an English language certification can help them access more opportunities. Most common English tests, such as TOEFL and IELTS, are expensive and require traveling to a test center. Businesses, schools, and other institutions started accepting Duolingo's certificate as a TOEFL equivalent. This meant more language learners could get certified, get better jobs, and generate more revenue for Duolingo.

By 2017, Duolingo's main revenue stream was the Test Center, but more money was needed, so they added ads. However, ads appeared at the end of the lesson, not in the lesson, so they wouldn't distract the learner. They also launched a paid subscription plan that removed ads and allowed users to download lessons onto the web or mobile platforms for offline usage. Another change to the business model. They grew to 200M users with 25M monthly active users. They created an internal Test Service, which had run over 2000 experiments by January 2020.

Where do they go from here? They could go back into B2B translation. They could go into other markets that need translation services like travel. How they continue to evolve their business model is a forever question, as it is for any company.

Duolingo Tests "Everything."

They often run hundreds of tests a week. A/B testing is one of their key testing methods that informs product decisions and roadmap. To scale their experiments consistently, Duolingo ensured each experiment had a hypothesis, expected outcome, links to related work, target audience, design, and interaction specifications.

First, different experiments affect different metrics, so the report outlines which metrics are relevant along with some universal metrics that are always included in the experiment so it would not negatively affect the learning experience or decrease engagement. The Test Service analyzes and creates reports for all running experiments every night.

Of course, not all experiments are successful or turn out as expected. For example, Duolingo tested a feature that allowed users to download lessons for offline usage. The experiment let users select learning offline and get an ad to buy Duolingo Plus when they tried to start the lesson. Users signed up for Duolingo Plus at a higher rate. But, even though revenue increased a little, retention dropped. The UI/UX of the experiment did not encourage users to use the app offline, which led to a decrease in daily active users. While the experiment was a success in terms of increased revenue, it wasn't in terms of DAU, so they didn't implement it.

Duolingo's testing service is critical to its success. Since so much of their testing is automated, people can focus on improving Duolingo and applying the insights to future iterations and experiments. The data also provides a continuous pipeline of user behavior.

Duolingo is also great at learning from those tests. It is important to document what you learn so that you don't repeat mistakes and can share the wisdom with others.

Create a learning template to track what each experiment has taught us. From running an experiment, you gain insight into your hypotheses. These insights include validation of your hypothesis by the evidence, invalidation from the evidence, new insights you didn't have before, or fuzzy insights you're still trying to figure out. If the evidence supports your hypothesis, keep going. If the evidence doesn't support your hypothesis, you have a few options - you can retest, pivot, or kill it. If you have new insights, you may want to pivot. If the insights aren't clear, retesting may help.

For example, Duolingo hypothesized that the copy for Spanish learners should be warmer and more encouraging if they quit a lesson before completing it. Putting it together:

1. **Hypothesis:** We believe the copy for Spanish learners should be warmer and more encouraging if they quit a lesson before completing it to help encourage, not discourage them.
2. **Observation:** Changing the text from "Do you want to end this session?" to "Don't give up! Do you want to end this session?" did not result in any change in users spending more time on lessons and quitting less often, as we had thought.

3. **Learnings & Insights:** From that, we learned that using warmer and more encouraging copy phrasing didn't affect Spanish learners' lesson completion rate.
4. **Decisions and Actions:** Therefore, we will examine other ways to increase lesson completion for Spanish learners.

For German learners based on the cultural data Duolingo had, they discovered that German learners didn't opt into push notifications, even though it can make it easier to develop a habit of learning.

1. **Hypothesis**: We believed that the copy for German learners needed to state the impact of notifications explicitly.
2. **Observation**: Changing the copy from "Duolingo needs to send you notifications" (which didn't explain why and what impact notifications had) to "Notifications are proven to foster learning success!" increased notification opt-in by 8%.
3. **Learnings & Insights**: From that, we learned that being direct and explicit in stating the benefits of notifications increased the use of notifications for German learners.
4. **Decisions and Actions:** Change the copy.

Now you know how testing can help you make decisions, we will dive into how you can develop your tests in the next chapter.

Sharpen Your Strategy

Pick a project. Start listing your key make-or-break hypotheses and consider how you can test them.

CHAPTER 11
DEVELOP EFFECTIVE HYPOTHESES FOR YOUR BUSINESS

We now know why testing is critical and how a streamlined process can help. We will use the Test Card, developed by my friend Alex Osterwalder, to make it easier. The Test Card has four key components: hypothesis, experiment, metrics, and criteria.

To run tests, you need to determine the types of hypotheses you are testing, how much evidence you already have, and how much time you have before you run out of money.

To start, you need to identify what **must** be true for your idea/venture to work. Can you break them down into smaller hypotheses, making testing easier?

We can categorize hypotheses into the following three types:

1. **Desirability:** Do people want this?
2. **Feasibility:** Can we physically make this?
3. **Viability:** Will we make a sustainable profit?

I recommend stating your hypothesis with "We believe" and starting with the desirability test. Because if your product isn't desirable, there's no need to create a business model.

Elements Of A Good Hypothesis

First, a good hypothesis is testable. A good hypothesis has to be able to be validated or invalidated based on evidence from testing, not on gut feeling. For example, take the hypothesis, "We believe Gen-X parents want services to help their kids get into the best colleges and universities." This is not a good hypothesis - what are the 'services' described? If you don't know what they are, how do you test them?

In contrast, "We believe Gen-X parents will hire higher-ed sports pros to help their middle school children identify and excel in the right sports for elite college and university recruitment" is a good hypothesis because it's testable!

Second, a good hypothesis is precise. Your hypothesis needs to describe exactly who, what, and when you are testing. For example, "We believe Gen-Z likes pop-up stores over store branches" is not a good hypothesis because it doesn't specify what kind of pop-up stores, products, or locations.

In contrast, "We believe that adults between 18-24 will spend more time in a household-essentials pop-up store in co-working spaces versus traditional store branches" is a good, precise hypothesis. Being precise with your hypothesis will help you identify a clearer market to target and pursue.

Finally, a good hypothesis is specific. Your hypothesis should have one specific idea to test. For example,

- Not Specific: We believe we can create an online service for Gen-X parents to find resources to help their children with college sports recruitment.
- Specific: We believe we can personalize a match of Gen-X parents making more than $200,000/yr and their middle school children with higher-ed sports pros for $1200 (our cost).

- Not Specific: We believe our digital platform helps us increase conversion rates and save money in call centers.
- Specific: We believe our digital platform will help us increase conversion rates by 5% AND help us save $200M in 3 years for call centers.

A specific hypothesis uses specific amounts, outputs, results, and outcomes - like paying $1200 for the match or a 5% increase in conversion rates.

Elements Of A Good Test

At the beginning, test as quickly and cheaply as possible. You want to run a few different types of experiments to increase the strength of the evidence.

At the same time, you want to choose the experiment that provides the strongest evidence you can afford. You want to get the best evidence possible to reduce uncertainty and risk. Strong evidence comes from real facts or events, as opposed to opinions or beliefs, and from observing what people do rather than what they say they do. Remember, you want to reduce the level of uncertainty as much as possible before you start building the product.

Combining levels of evidence with sample sizes makes the evidence more reliable and credible. Customer interviews with only ten people are pretty weak. A survey for discovery with 500 people is a little better. A simulated sales test with 250 people is pretty strong. I recommend doing various tests of the same hypothesis.

Take Strategyzer, founded by Alex Osterwalder, for example. Due to COVID-19, they had to go virtual, so they tested how well virtual masterclasses would work and what they could charge. Here's how they tested:

- The first hypothesis was about a new service: "We believe

people will attend a virtual masterclass."
- o Test: To verify this, we will send an email campaign, with three price points, to a pre-existing email list of people interested in Strategyzer masterclasses.
- o Metric: Measure the conversion rate of people who click on the email's call to action.
- o Criteria: We are correct if 2% of those who received the email clicked on the call to action, regardless of the price.
- The second hypothesis was about pricing: "We believe people will pay $1900 to attend a virtual masterclass."
  - o Test: To verify this, we will ask the same pre-existing email list of people to sign up for the Virtual Master Class (VMC) mailing list on three separate landing pages. The only difference between the three pages is the price - $1300, $1600, $1900.
  - o Metric: Measure the conversion rate of people who clicked on the sign-up call to action for the three different price points.
  - o Criteria: We are correct if the page with the highest sign-up rate is the price point closest to $1900.

What did these experiments cost to run? They were a combination of an email campaign and an A/B split test. The cost was $0.00 because the email lists already existed! The strength of evidence was about 60% (three out of five), and setup time took about 10 hours to design the experiment, draft the email and landing pages, build the email and landing pages, implement the test, and review the data. The runtime for the test was 48 hours - since email is fast, most people opened it within or around two days of receipt. The results were:

	$1300	$1600	$1900
Email with Virtual Class Announcement	1000	1000	1000

Number of emails opened	310	290	300
Number of clicks on email CTA	24 (2.4%)	30 (3%)	30 (3%)
Number of clicks on landing page CTA	9 (0.9%)	8 (0.8%)	19 (1.9%)
Number of Thank You form	8	7	11

For the first hypothesis: "We believe people will attend a virtual masterclass," they found that 3% clicked on the $1600 and $1900 prices.

What did they learn? The evidence supports the hypothesis. What decisions should they make? They can proceed with this idea because they are headed in the right direction.

Learning	Value
Hypothesis	We believe people will attend a virtual masterclass
Observation	About 3% of email recipients clicked on the email CTA, which indicates interest in a virtual masterclass
Learnings & Insights	Evidence supports the hypothesis!
Decision & Actions	Keep Going! We're headed in the right direction

For the second hypothesis: "We believe people will pay $1900", what did they learn? The evidence supports the hypothesis. Now, they can charge $1900 for virtual classes, which is the same as in-person ones.

Learning	Value

Hypothesis	We believe people will pay $1900
Observation	Group C ($1900) has the highest conversion rate of 1.9% out of 1000, compared to 0.9% for group A ($1300) and 0.8% for group B ($1600)
Learnings & Insights	Evidence supports the hypothesis!
Decision & Actions	Keep going! We can charge the same price for virtual as in-person!

You want to measure the number of unique views and unique sign-ups for landing page tests. For a video that explains your offering, you want to measure the number of unique views, number of shares, number of comments, and the click-through rate (ideally at 2%). If you're crowdfunding, metrics like the number of unique views, comments, and social shares have medium evidential strength. In contrast, metrics like the number of pledges, amount of dollars, and percent of total funding goal reached provide solid evidential data.

With the Test Card, you have learned how to develop a good hypothesis, set up reasonable experiments, and use learnings to drive actions.

◆ ◆ ◆

Sharpen Your Strategy

Make a list of the top five hypotheses that can make or break your project, new product, or venture. Then, identify the criteria you will use to determine success and how you will measure it.

CHAPTER 12 RUN A/B TESTING

Duolingo excels at testing. Everyone, including product managers, engineers, designers, and marketers, is empowered to propose and run a test. In this chapter, we'll learn how Duolingo built its testing culture and implemented A/B testing in their company.

Duolingo tracks results within established guardrails. They have a dashboard that shows how each test impacts key metrics versus a control group. If the results are positive, the feature can be shipped. However, if user engagement or retention is negatively affected, you need the senior executive or C-suite's sign-off.

"Test Everything" is one of Duolingo's core operating principles. To create a culture of experimentation, you need to develop a robust, repeatable process that drives continuous improvement and innovation. The system needs to be as objective as possible, and each experiment needs to be based on clear performance metrics and a large user base. Do you have a critical mass? What is the key metric you are optimizing for?

A culture of experimentation does not come cheap. You need to invest in a robust testing system. In the beginning, Duolingo used a third-party tool to manage experiments and later built their platform with the realization of how critical testing was to their business model.

Given this insight into how Duolingo embeds testing and experimentation into their culture, let's dive into four A/B tests that Gina Gotthilf, VP of Growth at Duolingo, thinks are most critical to their success in her own words.

These four critical A/B tests are

1. Delayed Sign-up
2. Streaks
3. Badges
4. A cute Owl to coach you along the way.

I put these in the Test Card format to help you apply the Test Cards.

For Delayed Sign-up, the hypothesis is "We believe that letting users try a lesson without having to sign up first will increase sign-ups."

1. To verify this, we will change the design of certain pages. They examined page designs and realized that the big red button that said "Discard my progress" was interpreted by users as "Don't Sign Up". Most humans tend to press the biggest button on a screen automatically, so this design might have led potentially interested users not to sign up. They redesigned the button, not in red anymore, and relabeled it to "Later." They called this tool for delaying the decisions 'soft walls' - optional pages that asked users to sign up but let them keep doing the lesson by pressing "Later."
2. And Measure: Increase or decrease in DAUs (Daily Active

VALUE PROPOSITION

Users).

3. We are right if DAUs increase by more than 1% and key metrics increase by 20-30% (with a baseline of 100K DAUs being statistically significant).
4. Result: Launch of Delayed Sign-up: In the first test, where the sign-up screen was moved back several steps, there was a 20% increase in DAUs. All of these tests, optimizing hard and soft walls, further increased DAUs by 8.2%. Instead of putting up a hard wall that forced a sign-up, it turned out that a few soft walls encouraged people to sign up more.
5. The lesson? You wouldn't know whether signing up before or after is better until you test it. It's valuable to test different combinations of soft and hard walls and see what you learn.

For Streaks gamification, the hypothesis is "We believe gamifying Duolingo will make it easier to retain users, keep them taking lessons, and make it more fun."

Studies have shown that the best way to learn a language is to study it daily, but for most people, that's hard.

1. To verify this, we will run several tests using different methods, notifications, wordings, and frequencies for users to keep track of how many days in a row they use the app. The Duolingo team experimented with "Streaks," the concept of tracking how many days in a row you use the app. The team tested different elements, including how a user sets a goal, when a user gets notified, and what the notification message looks like.

2. And Measure: How many days in a row a user uses the app (a key metric for user retention and DAUs)
3. We are right if: DAUs increase by more than 1% and key metrics increase by 20-30% (with a baseline of 100K DAUs to be statistically significant).
4. Result - Streaks: One key finding is that timing matters. They discovered that a notification 23.5 hours after the user started their last lesson worked - and it's worked ever since! Another key finding is that copy matters. They tested funny, serious, and urgent messages or quiz-like formats. They started using Duo, the Duolingo Owl Mascot. Duo's "Hi, it's Duo" notification was a hit and increased DAUs by 5%!
5. Most apps want users to develop a habit of using the app. The lesson? You can encourage users to set goals at the beginning of their app usage and help them do that by making it easy. The goals can change but put a stake in the ground. Then, you can create more meaningful notifications and emphasize notifying them just a tad before 24 hours after they last used the app. Tests can build on each other, and one test usually leads to more tests.

For Badge Rewards, the hypothesis is "We believe rewards for lesson completion will make learners complete more lessons more often."

1. To verify that, we will conduct several tests of various badge types and designs: The team had to remember the difference between getting a reward for simply showing up instead of accomplishing something. What kind of

rewards do users want? It turned out users didn't want rewards for just logging in; they wanted rewards for succeeding in the app! The new test involved several badge types and designs with an in-app location to show off the badges. Duolingo needed to avoid scope creep and decide what was in and out of the test instead of testing everything. They had 70 badge ideas and trimmed ideas through a design sprint.
2. And Measure: Increase or decrease in DAUs and percent of lessons completed.
3. We are right if DAUs increase by more than 1% and key metrics increase by 20-30% (with a baseline of 100K DAUs to be statistically significant).
4. Result - Badges: Implementing Badges was a significant resource investment; was it worth it? It turned out it was. With the first version of badges, DAUs increased by 2.4%, session starts increased by 4.1%, and lessons completed increased by 4.5%. Users started and finished more lessons because they wanted a badge! In addition, Duolingo store sales increased by 13%, and friend referrals increased new users by 116%! Users wanted to compete with their friends. Badges were a huge success!
5. This testing showed Duolingo the balance between an MVP that does just a little something versus doing everything. Putting product managers and designers together at the start helped sort features faster and counterbalance each other. The results of DAUs, session starts, completions, store purchases, and referrals show just that!

For Duo, the Owl Mascot, the hypothesis is, "We believe, based on behavioral psychology, that people are more encouraged by praising their effort versus their innate intelligence."

1. To verify that, we will see if Duo, the owl mascot, can encourage users to keep going: When users made a mistake, Duo popped up and said, "Even when you're making mistakes, you're learning." The team tested Duo saying, "Whoa, you're amazing!" vs. "Wow, your hard work is really paying off!" with the latter as the winner.
2. And Measure: Increase or decrease in retention
3. We are right if Retention increases by more than 1% and key metrics increase by 20-30% (with a baseline of 100K DAUs to be statistically significant).
4. Result - Duo, the Owl: Duo the Owl led to a significant % increase in user retention of 7.2% by day fourteen. Duo coaching users within the app was almost as successful in increasing user retention as badges!

Now, you have learned the key to building an experimentation culture and running A/B tests in the real world. While you may have a hunch on what will lead to growth, you need to build and enhance your product using data from real tests, not your hunch. And remember, product optimization often has more to do with the little things.

❖ ❖ ❖

Sharpen Your Strategy

What needs to happen to create a culture of experimentation on your team? Who would need to take the lead? What behaviors should be incentivized or de-incentivized? How could you reward experimentation and encourage learning from it?

CHAPTER 13
EXPERT INSIGHT
OF NONPROFIT

An Interview with Charlene Wang, founder of Distillable and LivingOS

Charlene Wang is the founder of Distillable and LivingOS.

In this interview, we talk about Charlene Wang's innovative approach to building a life-coaching community with LivingOS.

Deb Mills-Scofield: Could you share with us the genesis of LivingOS?

Charlene Wang: My journey began with a series of exploratory experiments within the startup ecosystem. I'm deeply passionate about helping founders and wanted to identify areas where I could offer substantial value.

Initially, I conducted office hours for founders, guiding them from the nascent stages of their ideas to the complexities of fundraising. I organized fifty 30-minute sessions, probing with questions like, "What does your ideal day entail?" and "Where do you see yourself a year from now?"

These interactions illuminated common challenges and potential solutions. Eager to streamline this process for scalability, I experimented with reducing the duration of these sessions. I conducted another fifty meetings, this time each lasting 20 minutes, to test whether I could achieve similar breakthroughs in a shorter time. Subsequently, I halved the duration to 10 minutes and, after 50 more sessions, found that this timeframe was sufficient to help individuals overcome their obstacles.

Deb Mills-Scofield: The crux of your methodology was adhering strictly to these time constraints—30, 20, and then 10 minutes—to maintain the integrity of your data. You essentially conducted 150 office hours, akin to customer interviews, to uncover people's needs, pains, and goals. This iterative process was key to validating your hypothesis.

Let's frame your office hours experiments using the Test Card model to better understand how you progressively determined the optimal session length and its impact.

1. **Hypothesis:** You posited that in sessions of 30, 20, or 10 minutes, you could assist founders in addressing their queries and delineating subsequent actions.
2. **To Verify This:** You engaged founders with open-ended questions ranging from "What does your perfect day look like?" to "What are your aspirations for the coming year?"
3. **And Measure:** Whether, in responding to these questions, founders could transcend their daily routines, identify their fundamental values, and utilize these insights to make a decisive choice with clear next steps.
4. **You Were Right If:** After 50 sessions of 30, 20, and 10 minutes each, you could discern and aid participants in achieving epiphanies that significantly altered their working methods – essentially, an "Aha!" moment.

Charlene Wang: Our journey began by forming a foundational community from individuals deeply passionate about personal growth. The insights gained from one-on-one interactions were pivotal. They fueled our intuition in crafting services and products that resonated deeply with our audience. To further harness these insights, we established a personal advisory group of high achievers. This group quickly evolved into a self-supporting network, with members actively sharing and addressing their challenges daily.

Deb Mills-Scofield: Starting with this minimum viable community as your initial offering, how did you expand to develop new products?

Charlene Wang: The key was our engagement with the community members right from the outset. Prior to developing anything, we were in constant dialogue with them. Our weekly group coaching sessions were instrumental in uncovering the common struggles and aspirations of the community. We observed a prevalent sense of uncertainty and confusion about personal goals. People were seeking guidance for their forthcoming decisions—a need I could deeply relate to.

Recognizing the limitations of existing mentorship structures, we identified an opportunity for improvement. Traditional mentorship programs often lacked the necessary framework to ensure success for both mentors and mentees. Mentees struggled with articulating their queries and maintaining engagement, while mentors were eager to contribute but lacked a reliable platform.

Our strategy included forming partnerships with communities that had already conducted thorough vetting. We chose to concentrate on the Asian American demographic initially due to the shared experiences and background within this group. A critical component of our approach was setting explicit expectations for mentor-mentee interactions—specifically, arranging three meetings over a three-month period.

To gauge the effectiveness and impact of our mentorship program, we relied on two key metrics: achieving a Net Promoter Score of at least 70 and maintaining high engagement levels. These indicators helped us assess the depth and significance of the connections fostered through our mentorship initiative.

Deb Mills-Scofield: You probed deeply with questions and genuinely empathized with the pains and aspirations of your audience. Through a series of empirical experiments, you were able to pinpoint and validate these needs. Let's lay this out in in a structured format:

1. **Hypothesis:** You hypothesized that a structured mentorship program would enhance the value derived by both mentees and mentors.
2. **To Verify That:** You honed in on a specific, underrepresented group - Asian Americans. You selected participants from well-vetted communities and established a clear expectation of monthly meetings over a quarter.
3. **And Measure:** Success was measured by the number of applicants, quality of matches, and the efficacy of the interactions.
4. **You Were Right If:** An NPS of at least 70 was achieved, alongside positive feedback on individual sessions, and if participants found the relationship valuable enough to continue beyond the initial three months.

The NPS is a crucial metric, reflecting the genuine customer experience through their likelihood of recommendations. A score above 70 is commendable, while over 90 is exceptional. Could you share the insights gained from this experiment?

Charlene Wang: The experiment confirmed our belief in the importance of structured interactions. This insight became a cornerstone of our core offering - the LivingOS Fellowship. To ensure the Fellowship's efficacy, we integrated the successful elements from our previous endeavors - personalized office hours, group coaching, and community mentorship. Constant iteration was key throughout this process.

Deb Mills-Scofield: Given that the Fellowship was constructed upon these validated learnings, its success was almost a foregone conclusion. Each aspect of the experience had undergone rigorous testing. Notably, you commenced with a specific demographic focus, which likely influenced the program's effectiveness. The relevance of the mentors' and mentees' generational backgrounds is an intriguing consideration.

Broadly, your experimental approach can be categorized into two segments - discovery and validation.

1. Discovery Experiments: These are foundational, aimed at testing initial hypotheses and assumptions, like your 30/20/10-minute office hour sessions.
2. Validation Experiments: These tests confirm the direction of your venture, exemplified by the development of the LivingOS community and fellowship.

For entrepreneurs, the choice of tests is contingent on the stage of their venture, a critical consideration for effective strategy implementation.

◆ ◆ ◆

Sharpen Your Strategy

Now think about your venture. What kind of tests can help you discover and validate your offering?

CHAPTER 14
STRATEGIZE WITH PRENATAL AND POST-MORTEM

The data on start-ups' rates of success and failure leads to a general rule of 10s, which I can validate as a VC: about 1 out of 10 start-ups succeed. Is there a way to increase those odds? Who knows at the macro level, but there are ways at the micro level. There are ways to reduce the risk of failure by thinking through all the possible things that could go wrong ahead of launch and testing for them. If you don't do that, you should at least go through everything that went wrong after the fact and learn from those, so you don't make those same mistakes again.

Let's use Titanic to learn how to diagnose a failure. Despite its "unsinkable" reputation, the Titanic sank after colliding with an iceberg. The cause of its sinking has been debated ever since.

What was the problem? The Titanic sank because it hit an iceberg.

Why can an iceberg sink an unsinkable boat? The iceberg made a huge hole in the hull, which filled up with water and sank the boat.

Why did the iceberg have such a severe impact on the boat? The hull could have been designed differently to control this, and steel strength could have been increased. The boat's speed could have been controlled by not going so fast.

Why did it hit an iceberg? The Titanic's captain had been warned about the icebergs from several sources, including a boat that had stopped for the night for that very reason and was only a few miles away (which raises the issue of why they didn't come to the Titanic's rescue).

Why did so many people die? The Titanic did not have enough lifeboats. Why? As originally designed, the boat required 64 lifeboats, cut in half and then in half again because the cruise line thought too many lifeboats would clutter the first-class passengers' views. In addition, the crew wasn't properly trained on how to use some of the lifeboat launch equipment, so it took longer than it should have when needed.

So now you can see why asking WHY five times can help you find meaningful solutions and create the needed changes. Simply saying that the Titanic hit an iceberg and sank, while factual, isn't enough to make sure it doesn't happen again.

There is much more to discuss regarding what went wrong, why it went wrong, how it could have been prevented, and how some things were prevented while others were not. That's why I chose the Titanic as an example to discuss planning and strategizing with prenatal and post-mortem methods in a business.

Prenatals help you identify all the potential risks and hypotheses that could go wrong ahead of time. You can refine the hypotheses, even turn your potential risks into clear, precise hypotheses, and thoroughly test them. This doesn't mean everything will be perfect, but it greatly reduces your risk of failure.

Post-mortems help you learn from what went wrong and avoid repeating those same mistakes.

Prenatals

The goal of prenatals is to figure out everything that can go wrong with your experiment before you do it. You start by asking, "What can go wrong here?" A great way to do this is to **get a multidisciplinary team together** (product, design, ops, engineering, marketing, finance, HR) - because these people think about the project, product, and risks differently. The more eyes of varying backgrounds that look at a problem, the higher the odds you'll find nuances and develop more powerful solutions.

I would suggest making prenatal an intrinsic part of any project you do and doing them at various stages throughout the project. For instance, when testing features or services, ask what could go wrong, how/when/why/where it could go wrong, and what you can do to prevent or at least mitigate them. At every stage of decision-making in creating your venture, ask these questions, list potential risks and their probabilities, and include those in your tests and/or test evaluations. Don't limit this to just the product, but apply this to how you vet ideas, how you make things, how you hire, onboard, and fire. Apply this to all aspects of running your venture.

At a foundational level, your prenatal should start with the hypothesis. Do you have the right ones - the most important ones that need testing before you do much else? Are they specific?

Precise? Discrete? Measurable? Testable the way you have them written? Use the Test Card "We Believe..." format mentioned in the previous chapter.

Now that you've nailed down your hypotheses, start your prenatal session by identifying all your risks. Before you do the actual session, send everyone a description of the experiment. Ask everyone to poke holes in the experiment - what could go wrong, what's not clear, what could be confusing, what data could be confused with something else. Rip the test apart. Think of everything that could go wrong and write them down - those are your risks. Write down any tacit assumptions or hypotheses implied in the test's hypothesis. Then, ask them to send this to you a few days before the session. Take all that and analyze and aggregate the data. Distill it down to the most often cited risks, issues, and list them by frequency.

Post-Mortems

I am a firm believer in doing post-mortems regardless of how the experiment went. Most people think of them as something to do when things go wrong. But that means we leave a lot of great learning on the table. In a post-mortem, you get to reflect on the insights you gained, next steps, as well as analyze the root causes (the core reasons that things didn't go as well as planned) and tree causes (the core reasons things went as well or even better than planned).

Root Cause Analysis is the process of figuring out the core issues and problems so they can be fixed, instead of just looking at the symptoms and fixing those. Generally, you start by identifying and defining the problem - as specifically as possible (what, when, where, how, effect on goals). Then, discover potential causes - and causes of causes until you get to the root and then figure out some great solutions. You would often ask "WHY" repeatedly, at least five times.

Some examples are:

- Joe gets headaches a lot. Why? Well, he doesn't drink a lot of water, and dehydration can cause headaches. Why? His home office is in the attic, and there's no sink up there, so he doesn't get water often. Why? He's not good at taking breaks. Why? He's either in a flow or has back-to-back meetings. You could ask why again with the response that Joe is not good at managing his time. So what could Joe do? He could have a bunch of water bottles upstairs and maybe get a little fridge to put them in. That way, he would always have water.
- Sue broke her ankle in a soccer game. She took Advil to relieve the pain. Taking Advil relieves the pain but doesn't treat the ankle. It doesn't increase bone healing. The root cause is broken bones. Pain is the symptom, and the problem is a broken ankle. Solution? See a doctor, get a brace or wrap, and have patience.

Now, let's do a deeper dive into post-mortems. When things go right, I call it Tree Cause Analysis because the roots are so strong that they support some wicked cool growth above ground. In Tree Cause Analysis, you want to focus on what's going well, what's working, and why it's working, instead of all the "what's not." We learn so much from analyzing the positive as well as the negative.

When an experiment goes well and you get positive results, find out what you did that made this so. Was it dumb luck? Was it because your hypothesis was very specific, your experiment was on point, and your metrics were right?

Document and share what went right, what worked, and learn. How can you apply that learning to other things, projects, experiments, so more things can go well? What core skills, tools, talent, and processes made it go well, and how can you leverage and develop those in other areas and disciplines? How can you embed that mindset in your culture - one that is positive, collaborative, innovative, and delights the customer? This is simple but not necessarily easy for everyone. It takes some time, a willingness to be self-reflective, as a person, manager, organization, and commitment to developing those things that generate energy and excitement instead of draining it.

Sharpen Your Strategy

Reflect on some of the experiments you conducted before. What were the root causes of the issues you encountered? What were the contributing factors? What did you learn from these experiences? Did you share your learnings with others, and how did that impact your subsequent experiments?

CHAPTER 15 TEST FOR DESIRABILITY

I hope it didn't sound like everything is rosy if you do all that testing. You can still fail because we don't often hear about the ones that didn't make it. We glamorize entrepreneurship and success, but it's a hard, long, non-linear slog to success. Having been a venture capitalist, I know the rules of 10 very well. We may get 1000 deals, look at 100, invest in 10, and 1 pays off. Let's learn from a few of the classic failures today.

Honest Tea, founded by Seth Goldman in 1998, was created as a mission-based company - organic ingredients, Fair Trade Certified partners, and ethical practices. This mission-driven company went on to be very successful, despite all the odds against it. Honest Tea was worth many millions before it was sold to the big leagues and killed.

Seth started his own tea company, borrowed money, and launched Honest Tea, which appealed to folks who shopped at places like Whole Foods. Honest Tea was a success. So much so that in 2008, Coca-Cola bought 40% of it and the rest in 2011. Sales went from $71M in 2010 to $600M in 2021.

But sales were slowing as overall 'ready-to-drink' tea sales were slowing nationally. The market was increasingly competitive with new ready-to-drink beverages like kombuchas, cold brew coffees, and other 'healthy' drinks. Meanwhile, Coca-Cola had redone its tea brand strategy. They decided to focus on its Gold Peak and Peace Tea, which have the scale and profit potential, and stop making Honest Tea by the end of 2022.

Honest Tea's:

- Sales have been consistently dropping.
- Its consumer base has a significant overlap with Gold Peak.
- It's sold in single-serve glass bottles versus Gold Peak, which sells in multi-serve packages, which is better for home use.
- Its declining sales are mainly in the West Coast and Northeast, the same locations of their glass supply chain issues.
- Results didn't match Coke's focus on high-growth, high-ROI brands.

Would a prenatal have shown any of this? Yes, if done more recently, which suggests that companies should always conduct prenatals on their offerings. They would have known about declining sales and Coke's consolidation strategy since it was in the news. If they had known, what could they have done? Look at marketing campaigns to boost sales? Redo the formula that no longer attracts users? Look for investors to buy Honest Tea from Coke? This is what Seth Goldman is doing; he's relaunching Honest Tea as "Just Iced Tea." He can't use the Honest Tea brand since Coke is keeping Honest Kids. We'll see how this turns out.

New Coke, introduced in April 1985, was Coca-Cola's answer to consumers' increasing focus on health and increased purchasing of diet soda and non-soft drinks. This was not good for Coca-Cola's most popular product Coke. Pepsi had gotten people to like sodas a bit sweeter, so Coke thought they should change the Coke recipe to be a bit sweeter. Initial sales increased by 8%, but Coke, based in Atlanta, is huge in the South. People in the South drink it first thing in the morning instead of coffee. It was rumored that more than 40K people called or wrote to Coke saying how angry and disappointed they were that Coke would change the recipe. 79 days after its introduction, Coke said they'd bring the old formula back, branded as "Coke Classic." Within a few months, Coke was back to the best-selling sugar-based cola, over Pepsi.

How could this have caught the Coke leadership team by surprise? Didn't they know this would happen? Didn't they conduct taste tests and market trials? They conducted almost 200K blind taste tests in the USA and Canada with consumers. What they didn't understand, and therefore didn't test for, was the emotional bond Coke drinkers had with their Coke. They tested for taste but not preference. They didn't ask, "Hey, what would you think if we changed Coke's recipe for a new one?" Leadership underestimated the emotional bond people had with Coke. Who knew? Users did. Would a prenatal have caught this?

How Old Navy Increased Its Style

Americans are getting bigger, body shapes are changing, and clothing retailers are adapting. However, Old Navy's plus-size line sales dropped by almost 20%. In the fall of 2021, Old Navy launched a marketing campaign of inclusivity, but sales started dropping. In April 2022, with the CEO and president leaving after only two years, Old Navy said they'd pull the line from stores and only offer the clothing online. But other brands were and are doing great - they're growing and making millions. So what didn't Old Navy do right?

Old Navy put a ton of money and resources into creating its new plus-sized clothing line that would fit many body shapes. They had new supply chains that could make multiple sizes, and the product was the same price regardless of size. However, they didn't understand the inventory they'd need for these new sizes on a per-store basis. They also didn't appropriately resize the styles. The lack of resized styles meant the clothes had huge pockets, misshaped waistbands, and out-of-proportion styling. Stores quickly sold out of size Medium, ending up with too much XSmall or XLarge. This meant stores had to discount to sell off inventory significantly. It's the age-old economic principle of supply and demand, which is never easy for retail in general, especially when dealing with a wide range of sizes.

But apparently, the competition can do it. Another company, Universal Standard, has managed to scale operations. How? They focused on the most common size in America - size 18. They call size 18 "medium," while the rest of retail calls size 8 "medium." By making their middle size the most common size in the country, ordering the other sizes is much easier. They have built their business model around the real size of Americans, which led to profitability. Historically, Old Navy's most common size was a lot smaller.

Creating a supply chain to support sizes 00-30 was much harder to figure out. This was also an issue for Universal Standard, but instead of going from 14 sizes to 30 virtually overnight, Universal gradually increased the number of sizes offered while simultaneously analyzing demand. Initially, they provided sizes 10-28, then 6-32, and now 00-40. As Universal attracted smaller and larger-sized women, they could increase orders.

Patience is a virtue. Old Navy made a big splash in introducing the plus-sizes, but maybe they wouldn't have had so many unsold large-sized clothes if they had done more and for longer. Changing consumer behavior takes time.

Applying existing business and operating models to new products and services is not always a great idea. Honest Tea's growth plans, pre-Coke acquisition, might have been good for a company of their size and scope. When Coke bought them, the desired growth goals went from a small beverage company to an international, global, multi-billion dollar company's goals. What worked for Honest Tea as an independent company would not work for Coke. Coke didn't buy Honest Tea to be a small niche player.

With New Coke, Coke seemingly forgot the other factors influencing a buyer's decision. Perhaps 'old' Coke had been around so long that the product and marketing people didn't realize that it was no longer just taste but the entire experience, and therefore emotions, around starting your morning with a Coke. Using the same-old, same-old methods of assessing consumer interest didn't apply anymore.

For Old Navy, while they had sold some plus-sized clothes before, they didn't realize that the operating model working for their regular clothes wouldn't work for their plus-sized clothes. It's not clear if they even tested the operating model. Despite how easy it is to get lulled into thinking that what works for one thing will work for another, don't. Check and confirm your business or operating model will work.

◆ ◆ ◆

Sharpen Your Strategy

What would have needed to be true for a pre-mortem analysis to be successful in preventing these failures? Consider all aspects of the business, including the open-mindedness of management, employees' willingness to speak up without fear of repercussions, the type of data that would have needed to be available, experiments they should have run, and more. Think of all the tangible and intangible aspects of the business, industry, and management. Leave no stone unturned.

CHAPTER 16 AVOID CONFIRMATION BIAS

Most companies and startups have wishful users. Wishful users are the users you **want** (wish) to have - the ones who do things the way you want instead of how they do. That's why it is important to discover and validate users through testing. Wishful users don't spend real money on your stuff.

Remember Vine? Vine was founded in June 2012, bought by Twitter when they were four months old, and launched in 2013. It isn't around anymore. Why? If you don't make a profit, you don't last (well, usually). Why didn't Vine make a profit? Well, there are several reasons.

One reason is that they didn't have a compelling value proposition. It was created to be a micro-vlogging social media service - share your short videos with friends and family. (Didn't Instagram do that? That's one of the competitors Vine lost to). But after Vine launched, it became an entertainment platform where users consumed rather than created content. Vine's key customer was not the viewer, but the content creator who had to engage with the service constantly. This was key, and Vine blew it.

If content creators are your target market, you need to understand them. They are creative and want to share their art, thoughts, and opinions. Vine's six-second limit was too short to allow for that. Vine kept to the six-second timeframe longer than they should have. A minute, or even 30 seconds, would have been much better. Furthermore, content creators want to get paid for their content, but Vine didn't pay them. You could grow your audience on Vine, but you couldn't make money off your content on Vine, so you'd move to another platform and take your audience with you (which meant Vine lost viewers).

Monetization wasn't just the creators' problem but also Vine's. Perhaps because venture capitalists always want fast growth with fast returns, Vine didn't experiment much with monetization, which reminds me of BeReal. Top content creators could get sponsorships, but that money went to them, not Vine. Twitter bought a social media talent management company for monetization, but the agency couldn't get its clients to stay on Vine. The creatives kept moving to a better, more competitive platform.

Today, short-form videos are the trend on most platforms (TikTok, Instagram, Snapchat, Facebook, and YouTube shorts). Most people think Instagram's support for short videos started Vine's demise. There are other issues related to management talent and turnover. However, it comes down to a bad value proposition: not understanding who the customer is and, therefore not providing the services they want and need.

Now, what about TikTok? Vine is dead. TikTok is killing it - with more downloads than other social media platforms. Vine was the first with short videos, but sometimes, it's better to avoid being the first and instead learn from those who came before you.

TikTok has been successful in a more competitive environment than Vine.

The difference? TikTok doesn't view itself as a social media platform. For instance, I doubt TikTok views Instagram as a real competitor. TikTok is entertainment for the masses, not sharing stories with your friends. You could argue it's not just entertainment, but also DIY, news, and learning. TikTok is focused on product-market fit - various lengths of videos, remixes, live streams, creator monetization (donations within live stream), and ads.

This is also the first time a Chinese company has taken the Western consumer app world by storm. Bytedance is vested in TikTok, and Twitter dropped Vine when it got into trouble. Perhaps because it wasn't Twitter's core business? It may be because it's not as rich as Facebook or Google. Whether TikTok is here for the long haul, its future looks bright.

Could a prenup have uncovered this? It could have given the right people at the table to discuss it. But this wasn't a new problem even then: in 2012, monetizing social platforms was a problem. Twitter had yet to figure it out, and they bought Vine, perhaps thinking it would work without thinking it through.

Now, let's talk about a mega-funded startup with no shortage of money that failed spectacularly within one year of launch. Quibi was founded by two bigwigs in the tech and entertainment world - Jeffrey Katzenberg and Meg Whitman. Katzenberg was Chairman of Walt Disney Studios and co-founded DreamWorks Animation. Meg Whitman was an executive at Walt Disney Company, DreamWorks, Proctor & Gamble (Tide!), Hasbro (My Little Pony), eBay, and HP. They are not a shabby leadership duo. Quibi was going to disrupt the streaming world, letting people watch videos on the go in landscape and portrait mode. The duo lined up huge Hollywood names and raised almost $2B before Quibi even launched.

Right before Quibi launched, COVID hit. The concept of watching on the go was a no-go because no one was going anywhere. You could watch something longer since you were stuck at home. It had many problems in its mere 6-month existence: lawsuits, unhappy subscribers, lack of product features, and more.

Ultimately, I believe all companies fail because of poor management — the inability to understand the customer, to put ego aside, not understanding the supply chain, or the need to scale. These reasons boil down to humans. Katzenberg and Whitman didn't get what Quibi should be. Most people felt that Quibi's shows were lousy. The shows were ones that big Hollywood types hadn't been able to sell.

While COVID had an impact, you can't blame the lack of a compelling value proposition and no product-market fit on just a virus. Quibi did not allow screenshots or sharing of clips. Furthermore, it costs $5/month for lousy content or $8/month for the same lousy content but without ads. You could get a lot of that content for free or on platforms you already paid for.

Most importantly, no one ever answered the critical question — why should Quibi even exist? Why did people need Quibi? Perhaps things would have been different if Quibi had a breakthrough must-watch show. If you're on your phone and want to watch something, what app will you use? Netflix, TikTok, and maybe

Instagram. Not Quibi. Fundamentally, Quibi didn't know what the company was or what it should be. Some said that TikTok killed Quibi, but Quibi died partially because leadership didn't acknowledge TikTok in the first place. The result? Quibi shut down.

One obvious question I would have raised is: What will you do when COVID isn't an advantage to the business model? What will you do when people are out and about? A pandemic does not wholly make or break a value proposition or business model. Sometimes, having all the money you need is not a good thing. It doesn't force you to make hard decisions or prioritize resources and markets, and it can drive a sense of invincibility.

◆ ◆ ◆

Sharpen Your Strategy

Ask a friend who isn't close to your work critique it. See what they find challenging, and consider incorporating their feedback into a pre-mortem, so you don't have to perform a post-mortem analysis.

CHAPTER 17 REFINE YOUR TARGET MARKET

Odds are that your first date won't be "the one," the forever, soulmate kind of one. The same is true for customers. Odds are that your first customers, first users, will not be the ones that get you to whatever you've defined as success. This happens to a lot of startups and what are now big companies. Dropbox initially thought individual users were their golden goose because that's what got the founders thinking about Dropbox in the first place. But, in reality, it was small and large businesses that resonated enough with Dropbox's value proposition to pay for subscriptions. And yes, experimentation was critical.

Dropbox's pitch is legendary. There was no product, just a video of what Dropbox would do. Dropbox was founded in 2007 by Drew Houston. While at MIT, Houston kept forgetting to bring his USB drive to class, so he didn't have what he needed. The cloud-like services in 2007 were slow, buggy, and not meant for non-techie people. Dropbox is a classic founder story—Houston's job was having his data with him in class. The pain was forgetting to bring his USB (the data) with him. The gain would be having his data accessible without having his USB. Houston applied to Y Combinator (YC) and started getting noticed. His YC demo pitch was a video of what the service would do, not a demo of the service, but a video of what the service could be—a classic discovery experiment.

In 2008, Dropbox publicly launched with a private beta. The marketing for the initial launch used pretty typical experiments: buying Google Adwords, hiring a PR firm, affiliate marketing, and display ads, resulting in a CAC (Customer Acquisition Cost) between $233 to $400/user for a planned $99/yr subscription fee. There's a problem with the math. Only 5,000 people signed up for the pre-launch wouldn't cut it.

Dropbox felt they needed 10,000 beta users to validate their value proposition hypothesis: We believe that consumers understand the cost of storage, whether it's in the cloud or on a hard drive, so they will pay for Dropbox. Given the value proposition of data being available anywhere, anytime, Dropbox couldn't launch until they were 100% sure the service would work. Failure wasn't an option. The availability and security of beta users' files in the cloud had to be a given because beta users were REAL users. Dropbox was doing all the "standard" marketing that was supposed to get users, but they weren't getting users—at least as many as they wanted.

Back in 2008, cloud storage wasn't a big deal. People weren't searching for "document sync services" or "online storage," which meant keyword search analysis wouldn't help Dropbox assess market needs. While access to data anywhere was a problem for people, most didn't realize it was a problem.

Forget traditional marketing to get beta users. Dropbox went back to its successful YC demo video. They posted another video on Digg and Reddit, developer sites with potential early adopters.

Within hours, they got many Reddit upvotes and landed on Digg's front page. In 24 hours, Dropbox had 75,000 beta users, 15 times what it originally had. By the end of 2008, they had 200,000 registered users. Most were techies and typical early adopters they had wisely targeted to get their 75,000 beta users. This was fabulous, but Dropbox needed a wider user base to scale. Dropbox did another video aimed at more general, non-techie users. The video was about a guy who goes to Africa, needs his data, gets on Dropbox, and voila—data!

This video was a story about user's needs, not what a product did. This is a critical point I can't stress enough. The first video that got Houston into YC focused on the solution, and what Dropbox could do in terms of user jobs, pains, and gains. The second video focused on users' jobs, pains, and gains first, very clearly, and why Dropbox was the solution. This guy in Africa had a job that required access to data. His huge pain was that he didn't have his data with him, and the gain was he could always have his data. To test the response to this second video, they created a simple landing page with a clear download button and a clear call to action. It is critical to focus on the user—to truly understand your users' jobs, pains, and gains, instead of focusing on what your product does. There is an adage in the startup world—fall in love with the problem, not the solution. Dropbox raised a $6M Series A that year with major investors like Sequoia Capital.

Dropbox did a lot of A/B testing in the beta, honing page layout, content, and placement of display ads, including those that hid the freemium service level to see if people would sign up for the paid version. Dropbox's testing was much like Buffer's and Strategyzer's. The testing showed Dropbox that users wanted

Linux as well as Mac and Windows. Users loved Dropbox's reliability, dependability, simplicity, pricing, and messages on users' decisions to keep freemium or upgrade to a paid plan. This also resulted in Dropbox's decision to decrease the amount of free storage in the freemium plan.

Dropbox's next level of growth came from yet another classic experiment: referrals. In the first month, 2M invites were sent. When someone you referred signed up, you got free space. Referral became a huge success and part of the initial user onboarding process.

The key here was Dropbox's wording. They didn't say, "Invite a friend," which is the typical come-on for referrals. They said, "Get More Space," and let users know how their invites were doing. If they were getting real signups and hence, more space, the referral program experiment validated Dropbox's product-market fit. People wanted more space and were willing to spread the word to get it.

Remember how initially Dropbox thought individual users (B2C) were its target customers? Their initial hypotheses focused on syncing files across several devices, not sharing with others. Dropbox believed that:

- Users had multiple devices and wanted to access the same file(s) on any of those devices at any time;
- Accessing files across devices was hard;
- Users wanted to download the Dropbox app on their multiple devices;
- Users would trust Dropbox with their sensitive and important data;

- Users would understand Dropbox's file/folder structure;
- Dropbox could build a service that would let users sync all sorts of files across all sorts of devices and operating systems;
- Dropbox could build a syncing service that is very fast and 100% accurate.

The test result helped Dropbox discover a new target market. The initial hypotheses around users wanting to sync many types of files across various devices changed over time. Dropbox started to see that its most valuable users were not individual users, but users within a company who wanted to sync, share files, and collaborate on documents with people inside and outside their company. These people upgraded to higher tiers, paid for more storage, and used extra features. The revenue was coming not from B2C but from B2B! This told Dropbox that having a product-market fit for B2C meant a mostly freemium plan, which wasn't sustainable. But if they tailored Dropbox to include sync, file sharing, and collaboration services, users were willing to pay! These users were mainly people working at a company.

Since Dropbox wanted to go viral, they added the ability for Dropbox users to share files with non-Dropbox users without a referral. You just had to invite them to share a file. This took referrals to a whole other level. If you're considering using referral experiments in your venture, consider adding features like this to make it even more powerful and validating.

When Dropbox first launched sharing, the recipient didn't have to create a Dropbox account to access the shared Dropbox file. But eventually, Dropbox changed that. Sharing files increases the external network effects — the more people that are on the system, the more useful the system is because there are more people to work with, which increases the number of people who will sign up, further increasing the system's value. None of the other cloud storage services at the time allowed free collaboration.

Fast forward to 2023, Dropbox is viewed by many as a master of user testing and experimentation to discover, validate, and grow! They use their testing process to

1. Validate their current value proposition and discover its ongoing evolution. Their compelling value proposition consists of their world-class reputation and client list, the reliability and quality of their solutions, extremely high availability and reliable security and privacy, dedicated technical specialists, and solution flexibility and accessibility.
2. Grow their user base. They had 4M users and more than doubled their base from 2013 to 2014. In 2018, Dropbox became the first Y Combinator startup to file for an IPO. At the end of 2021, they had more than 700M registered users, 16.8M paying users, and 80% of the usage was for business. Revenues in 1Q22 were $562M globally.

◆ ◆ ◆

Sharpen Your Strategy

Take a look at your venture and consider the customer segments you have targeted or are targeting. Have they changed? Are you confident that these are the correct segments? How can you find out? What tests can you perform to validate the segments you have selected or to identify different, more valuable ones?

CHAPTER 18
CLIMATE INDUSTRY EXPERT INSIGHT

An interview with David Schurman, co-founder of Perennial

David Schurman is the co-founder and CTO of Perennial, recognized by Time Magazine among 2022's top 100 innovations.

Pivoting is an integral part of startup evolution, involving changing business models, target customers, products/services, or other aspects to adapt assumptions and align with growth.

In this interview with David Schurman, we dive into the founding story of Perennial. Initially focused on hyperspectral imaging, Perennial pivoted into soil-based carbon removal verification, becoming an industry leader.

Deb Mills-Scofield: Tell us how you got started with your company.

David Schurman: My two co-founders and I come from farming families and have always been passionate about climate and sustainability issues. We wanted to help farmers, so in 2018, we started exploring how hyperspectral imaging could detect crop diseases and nutrient deficiencies.

We began with a proof of concept, developing a machine learning system implemented on drones to test if we could detect crop health issues. When that worked, we transitioned to planes to cover larger areas at scale. We conducted test flights and proved we could image key crop nutrients like nitrogen, phosphorus, and potassium (NPK) over hundreds of acres. To validate the technology further, we compared the hyperspectral data to soil samples from the same fields.

Deb Mills-Scofield: How did you acquire your first customers?

David Schurman: We targeted agronomists and agricultural advisors as initial customers since their farmer clients could benefit. We wanted to demonstrate that our data helped advisors increase yields by targeting underfed areas and save farmers money by avoiding over-application in areas that didn't need more nutrients. Our initial model charged a per-acre fee for the data.

Deb Mills-Scofield: That pivot to focus on carbon was a big change. What drove that decision?

David Schurman: Our original nutrient detection technology, while valuable, didn't provide enough cost savings to justify purchase by cash-strapped farmers. We realized we needed a new business model to truly impact their livelihoods and the environment.

So we began exploring soil carbon sequestration - farmers could get paid for the carbon their soil captures. This represented a potential new revenue stream, more stable than fluctuating crop yields. It also offered greater environmental benefits.

Adding carbon detection to our system wasn't feasible, so given the need for new farmer revenue models and climate change, we decided to pivot to carbon fully. This created an entirely new income stream versus just optimizing an existing one.

Deb Mills-Scofield: After investing in the nutrient detection technology, that pivot must have been difficult. How did you scale the carbon solution?

David Schurman: We knew we needed to sample vastly more acres to scale. But planes weren't reliable enough, with weather and ground conditions impacting flyovers. So we pivoted to satellites, which orbit consistently. We supplemented our machine learning model with public NASA data, improving accuracy over planes. The satellites' consistent revisit times and calibration also helped. We could pick the best data from all available imaging.

Deb Mills-Scofield: With more accurate large-scale data, have your target customers changed?

David Schurman: Yes, we now provide insights on hundreds of thousands of acres at a time to food companies and others, analyzing supply chain climate impacts. Unlocking soil's carbon capture potential at scale creates the biggest supply of carbon credits in a constrained market. Our customers are now carbon developers and corporate offset buyers versus individual farmers and agronomists. Our mission remains to unlock soil as a carbon sink in a way that works for farmers.

Deb Mills-Scofield: Pivoting is inevitable for startups, though certainly not easy. The tendency is to keep trying to validate your original hypotheses instead of admitting they may be flawed. It takes courage, consensus, and collaboration to pivot - traits critical for any startup.

This willingness to pivot led Perennial to raise an $18 million Series A in May 2022. So David, what were the key hypotheses you tested to get where you are today?

David Schurman: We asked, "What must be true to scale impact and adoption at an acceptable price point?" First, we must help customers make money. Analyzing nutrient detection versus carbon opportunities showed carbon's greater revenue potential for farmers. Second, we need affordable technology. Despite the risks, we pivoted from expensive planes to more cost-effective satellites. Combining these factors led to a solution with a true impact on livelihoods and climate. Migrating software was tricky, so we balanced thorough testing with speed.

Deb Mills-Scofield: If starting over, would you do anything differently?

David: In hindsight, I wish we'd analyzed who else used planes for data. We'd have learned most rely on satellites due to the high cost of planes for marginal improvements in resolution. Satellite data combined with soil sampling was more cost-effective for scale.

Deb Mills-Scofield: What signals it's time to pivot?

David Schurman: A few user-focused factors. We found our original nutrient service, though valuable, wouldn't generate enough profitability for farmers in unpredictable markets. By listening, we learned supplemental revenue could be a win-win for them and the planet.

Assess how valuable your proposition truly is – can users pay over time, even in downturns? Have you targeted the right users? Can they live without what you offer? Evaluating these aspects of your value proposition can indicate whether it's time to pivot – rarely an easy call, but most startups do. It's part of learning and growth.

CHAPTER 19 SUSTAINABILITY INDUSTRY EXPERT INSIGHT

An interview with Ben Chesler, co-founder of Imperfect Foods

Ben Chesler co-founded Imperfect Foods in 2015. From COO to CTO to Head of Strategy, he served in numerous leadership roles during its rapid growth to over $500M in sales. After 5 years, Ben transitioned to the board and now advises social entrepreneurs on scaling their own mission-driven companies. Forbes named him one of the 30 Under 30.

In this interview with Ben Chesler, we discussed opportunity spotting, team building, validating markets, and redefining consumer norms.

Deb Mills-Scofield: Let's begin with the beginnings of Imperfect Foods. How did you first identify the potential for a business focused on recovering and selling aesthetically imperfect produce?

Ben Chesler: During a gap year in 2011, I volunteered with the Food Recovery Network (FRN) where I met co-founder Ben Simon. We attended conferences on food systems and learned the shocking statistics about food waste in agriculture - vast amounts of fruits and vegetables are left unharvested solely because they fail to meet retail cosmetic standards. Though the FRN began a small gleaning operation to recover some of this produce, the effort was discontinued as it wasn't viewed as core to the FRN's mission. However, I recognized consumer demand based on the enthusiastic response to our initial 700 orders per week. An FRN intern even launched a similar effort independently in Maryland.

A year later, confident in proof-of-market, Ben Simon and I decided to pursue what had previously seemed a "side project." Establishing a reliable supply chain posed the main challenge. However, a chance conference encounter resulted in connecting with Ron Clark, who already worked in produce aggregation. With supply secured and buoyed by the growing "ugly food" movement in Europe, Imperfect Produce (later Imperfect Foods) launched in 2015. The time was right to redefine beauty norms in food.

Deb Mills-Scofield: Securing reliable supply and demand is fundamental to any startup's success. With supply relationships established through Ron Clark, Imperfect Foods launched in 2015 as a small Oakland-based business focused on recovering ugly yet nutritious produce. However, proof-of-demand still needed validation. What customer acquisition strategies did you leverage to drive sign-ups and grow your subscriber base?

Ben Chesler: Our initial FRN gleaning endeavor and 700 weekly orders suggested product-market fit potential. Still, the Oakland region represented an unknown. We decided to test area demand through scrappy experiments that could demonstrate a sizable market existed.

First, we hired local high school students to sell Imperfect Produce subscriptions door-to-door. The value proposition was that subscribers would save money, get fresh, healthy produce, albeit perhaps ugly. Their youthful enthusiasm and our messaging converted many customers.

Next, we leveraged media relationships established during my

FRN days. Numerous food waste journalists helped spread Imperfect's mission through features in high-profile outlets like NPR and PBS. We were on the cover of the New York Times Food Section the day we launched, which had a snowball effect and resulted in over 20 media outlets copying the article.

Finally, referrals and word-of-mouth proved to be effective customer acquisition strategies. Through ongoing optimization over nearly two years, we doubled referral credits and identified key moments that drove advocacy. Sign-ups and first orders represented critical junctures for capturing customer attention with tailored digital and print collateral encouraging referrals. Further data analysis revealed that the third order marked a retention tipping point. We subsequently incorporated referral incentives at this moment.

Additionally, we leveraged Imperfect Foods' growing brand recognition to pilot cost-efficient ads targeted at relevant online communities. Despite initial concerns about authenticity, paid posts in moms' Facebook groups asking members to share with their networks showed promising results. We also became the first paid advertiser on Nextdoor.

This multi-channel approach helped convert early adopters into vocal advocates.

Deb Mills-Scofield: Now that supply and demand fundamentals were in place, how did initial customers respond to the Imperfect Produce offering, and what key learnings emerged from those early reactions?

Ben Chesler: We made several pivots during the first year based on customer feedback and behavior analysis.

Initially, we followed a community-supported agriculture (CSA) model with pre-set produce assortments. However, allowing no customization proved problematic. Customers began canceling subscriptions, fatigued by repetitive items like sweet potatoes in every box. This backhanded test revealed a divergence between our standardized operational approach and diverse consumer preferences.

Within six months, we introduced product personalization options despite added inventory, logistics and purchasing complexities. Enabling choice boosted satisfaction and retention, confirming the merits of a customer-centric strategy. When farms couldn't supply specific produce ordered, we even sourced market gaps locally to avoid substitutions. While inefficient, this practice ultimately reduced overall food waste by selling more varied and personalized produce.

Through iterative experimentation, we determined that complexity and customization created the most value.

Deb Mills-Scofield: Business model pivots like moving from set boxes to customization are challenging. As the company evolved from Imperfect Produce to Imperfect Foods, what key changes were involved in that product line expansion?

Ben Chesler: In 2019, we made the controversial decision to expand beyond produce into select grocery items. Two factors drove this strategy pivot:

First, Imperfect sought to further its mission of reducing food waste across the entire supermarket, not just the produce aisle. Data revealed substantial spoilage in categories like meat, dairy and nuts.

Second, analysis indicated the addition of staples like eggs and milk would better meet the needs of core customer segments like vegetarian subscribers. Providing a "one-stop shop" had the potential environmental benefit of consolidating trips to acquire groceries into a single delivery.

However, early execution challenges emerged:

1. Unlike imperfect produce, customers expect perfect condition meat, dairy and eggs. Sourcing standards had to be revisited.

2. Poor change management and messaging created confusion and skepticism over how new items aligned with Imperfect's brand and waste-fighting mission. Some employees even quit as a result.
3. We realized external assumptions can define a brand as much as its own narrative. For example, people inferred local sourcing and vegetarian orientation from our original produce-only focus, though neither claim was made explicitly.

In response, we rebranded from Imperfect Produce to the broader Imperfect Foods to realign perceptions with the expanded category focus. Additional steps were then taken to refine grocery integration according to customer preferences and values.

Deb Mills-Scofield: Please explain how you refined the grocery offering and communicated the changes after switching to Imperfect Foods.

Ben Chesler: We reorganized the business around:

1. Products with high food waste rates, based on data.
2. Our own private grocery label given customer perception issues regarding mainstream brands.
3. Clear sustainability guidelines for sourcing standards, especially for non-produce items.
4. Simplified produce and grocery bundles realigned to target customer values.

This focus on transparency, integrity and intentionality aimed to rebuild trust in our expanded mission. Messaging also centered on empowering customers to drive real-world impact, whether through enjoying an imperfect apple or crooked carrot. With every bite, shapes attitudes and behaviors for the better.

Deb Mills-Scofield: Shifting consumer norms is an arduous process, but offers great upside for bold entrepreneurs. Imperfect Foods provides lessons in redefining quality standards, developing supportive business models, and evolving mindsets around sustainability.

Since its early Oakland days, the company has rapidly grown to over 1,000 employees serving nearly nationwide demand. Other major players continue to recognize Imperfect's success in establishing ugly produce as the new normal, with a recent $700 million acquisition offer from grocery delivery competitor Misfits Market.

In closing, consider overlooked consumer segments, undervalued products being discarded, and outmoded assumptions to uncover your own opportunity to posit a new normal. The common ingredient across brands pioneering new standards is simply a willingness to question the status quo.

CHAPTER 20
ELIMINATE CHILDHOOD HUNGER

COVID-19 has presented significant challenges for businesses worldwide. Many companies have struggled to adapt to the rapidly changing landscape; some have even been forced to shut their doors permanently. Today, we'll learn about a business successfully managing these challenges.

Throughout the pandemic, the Second Harvest Food Bank of North Central Ohio (SHFB) has continued to provide food to those in need. Unlike most organizations, where it's all about growth and scale, food banks aim to put themselves out of business. Success is when everyone has enough food. SHFB's approach to putting themselves out of business is to meet increasing food needs and work with their communities and governments to eliminate the need for SHFB to exist.

Like any other business, food banks need to raise capital to do what they do: buy and give out food. The need for capital is especially dire due to rising inflation, as well as diseases and wars that affect the food supply chain. How did SHFB get food and money?

SHFB's business model relies on donations of food and money. While fundraising is hard work, SHFB has an extremely compelling value proposition for the region it serves. The thought of hungry children is hard to swallow. People see the need and give generously. However, when our world has disaster after disaster, people become overwhelmed. The depth of food insecurity is easily forgotten, so how has SHFB kept its mission and impact front and center?

To create a value proposition, you need to start with the user. Most food banks define food pantries as their users because that's who they give the food to, who distributes it to those in need. What are food pantries' jobs, pains, and gains? Food pantries are important in addressing hunger. But SHFB goes beyond that. They focus on the needs of the community members: the families, the people coming to the food pantry for food, and how the food pantries can get the food to community members. While this may seem like a subtle difference, it profoundly impacts changing the paradigm.

Here's why: If you only focus on the food pantries, you will not go into the communities and talk to the people in need. Some of the best experiments SHFB uses to discover and validate its hypotheses are customer interviews, Day-in-The-Life, surveys, and more. Since SHFB is always learning about its community members, they are always searching for the best way to meet their community members' needs.

Through those interviews, SHFB learned about the stigma of going to a food pantry. Volunteers and workers in pantries can be judgmental. "Well, she looks well-dressed." "Those kids don't look like they need food." When you hear those things, would you go get the food you desperately need? Knowing this stigma, SHFB knew they needed to change the traditional food distribution models before COVID.

The need for food always exists, but the way to deliver it is complex and ever-evolving. SHFB uses Appreciative Inquiry, which starts with the premise that communities have the assets - knowledge, skills, and desire - to create solutions for many of their challenges. They don't need people from the outside telling them what to do. SHFB walks alongside the communities to identify these assets and understand what the community is doing well and right. SHFB works with partners, such as local governments, agencies, community groups, and businesses, to create ways to reduce hunger. Partnerships also ensure these organizations have skin in the game. By experimenting and validating its hypotheses in these ways, SHFB has solved one of its biggest challenges: how to distribute food.

One of the biggest challenges with today's food pantry model is that the people who support food pantries are getting old. Many food pantries are closing and reducing their open hours. How many working families can go to a food pantry at 10 am?

SHFB was looking at ways to increase food accessibility and availability. Instead of saying, "We could use XYZ as a distribution pantry," they went into the communities to understand when and where the most convenient places for community members to get food were. Food should be available where single parents run errands and go regularly. SHFB looked at where community members were and figured out how to get the food there.

Remember, food banks don't distribute food directly to community members - that's the job of the pantries and partner charities. This approach drives a fundamental shift in the value proposition. It's about the community members, not those delivering the food.

After many experiments, SHFB ran pilots to validate how to get food to children in need. For example, SHFB validated that having food pantries in schools for kids to take food home at the end of the day meant reaching more community members in need. They also put pantries in public libraries, another central location community members frequented. Through the pilots, they learned more about what kind of food community members wanted and needed, as well as some obvious and more nuanced socio-demographic needs.

Building on the success of the school pantries, SHFB partnered with other organizations to reduce overall childhood hunger in

VALUE PROPOSITION

the region. In September 2019, just before COVID hit, SHFB held the Child Hunger Summit to bring stakeholders and partnership opportunities together.

Then COVID hit. If you want to learn how to be operationally, logistically agile, nimble, and pivot within 48 hours, be a food bank during COVID. The number of people in need grew exponentially. Pantries closed. Many volunteers were at risk. Getting food to the number of people in need seemed impossible.

Since it's COVID, SHFB only had front-line essential employees. SHFB partnered with the National Guard to streamline its operations and logistics and integrated the National Guard into the culture in a way few other food banks did. SHFB also received significant monetary donations to buy food, which, when coupled with the workforce of the National Guard, enabled them to scale mobile drive-through pantries at easily accessible locations using safe COVID protocols.

SHFB also took on mobile pantries as another necessary direct distribution channel. SHFB quickly set up a no-touch registration process and had tents to protect perishables from the weather. In 2020, in just one week, 13,000 households were served. 30,000 households were served in a month. Over 14 million pounds of food were distributed in less than a year. Don't ever doubt the reality of food insecurity.

Eventually, the National Guard was called back from duty at the food banks. The loss reduced SHFB's ability to deliver food at the same pace in the same quantities. However, food insecurity is even higher after COVID, with inflation and supply chain issues.

Many volunteers returned, and SHFB still serves 10-12 mobile pantries a month. SHFB is considered the organization that pulls community organizations together, public and private, to solve real problems. This is a testament to the SHFB team's character, integrity, and determined focus. They stay true to their mission by partnering with public and private stakeholders, which builds sustainability, accountability, and strength.

While many of the fellow food banks in Ohio are shutting down, SHFB still depends on innovation to survive. SHFB will keep delivering on its value proposition and feeding those in need in ways we have yet to create. In the meantime, if you're wondering what types of pressing problems you could create a company to address, consider making a real impact on the people and community around you.

Sharpen Your Strategy

How can you apply the approach of the Second Harvest Food Bank to design sustainable solutions for your own business?

CHAPTER 21 BUILD A HYPOTHESIS-DRIVEN CULTURE

For many people today, how we define work is an open-ended question. We can work for companies of all sizes, industries, locations, and business models. We can work for ourselves as freelancers, and start our own ventures. There are no right or wrong answers. You can change them at any time.

If you're doing a startup, why? What drove you to do this? What made you know you had (or wanted) to take this path? What functional, emotional, psychological, and/or social jobs does being an entrepreneur fulfill for you? Is it the freedom to be your boss and have more control? Is it a product or service you feel you must make because of the difference it will make in people's lives? Is it because that's what you've been told you 'have' to do? Is it because all your friends are starting ventures?

I hear you saying, "Deb, enough with the questions already!" But it's important to understand why you're doing, or want to do, a startup because it's not an easy road, and at times it's lonely, even with a great team. Please take the time to reflect on these questions and create your own value proposition:

1. What are the specific jobs that this venture fulfills for you? Just as it's a critical question to understand for your potential customers, it's as essential to ask for yourself.
2. What are the pains you're trying to alleviate for yourself? What are the pains that you're trying to avoid or mitigate by doing your own venture? These could be things like having to report to someone, not feeling in control, not working on what you want to work on, not having the impact you'd like to have, not being able to physically be where you want to be, not being able to work with the people you want to work with, etc.
3. What do you gain by starting your own venture? Freedom, financial success, prestige, credibility, reputation, the ability to change lives, or something else?

One of the most critical skills for successfully building a compelling value proposition, and thus a business, is learning to ask great questions. It's not just about finding one answer because there are often many answers. And the answers you get are determined by your questions and how you ask them. That's why using multiple forms of testing is so important because it helps reduce potential bias. In today's highly competitive and fast-paced world, those who can learn and apply the fastest will succeed and make an impact. You do that by questioning everything objectively, honestly, and civilly. Don't stop being curious.

Culture matters. Culture, which must come from leadership, drives how decisions are made, employees are treated, and customers are prioritized—all of which drive financial results. If your ego is too big, it will affect who you listen to and how you make decisions. If you don't leave the office or building, you can easily lose touch with customers and those who helped you succeed. It's easier than you think to get swept up in the whirlwind. Stay humble.

Most of the corporate world loses the intense focus on continually testing their value propositions, especially as they become more and more successful. The biggest inhibitor to success is success. It drives complacency, inward focus, and losing touch with your customers.

Think back to Buffer in the earlier chapter. Buffer's leadership has relentlessly stayed curious and humble and tested everything they do with their employees and customers. Do they have ups and downs? Yes, but the focus on being hypothesis-driven makes for a more sustainable business overall.

A hypothesis-driven culture does not mean you are slow to make decisions or get products to market. Although it seems paradoxical, you can be hypothesis-driven and fast. Constant experimentation means you're learning, applying that learning, and getting products out to market. Hypothesis-driven companies know how to balance validation and speed. They learn all the time, so they learn fast and can apply fast. They have a learning infrastructure with strong learning muscles based on experience. They are a place people love to work in and a place where the business is always growing.

CONCLUSION

Designing a Winning Strategy for Your Company

One should evaluate one's company from a strategic perspective.
1. Conduct listening sessions with each department lead.
    1. Perform an annual retrospective.
        1. How did the team perform relative to quarterly objectives?
        2. How did the team function holistically based on 360 feedback?
    2. When reviewing, look for the following:
        1. Is there an open culture where employees feel comfortable speaking openly?
        2. Does leadership have sufficient data to understand company performance fully? Are adequate assessment mechanisms in place? A comprehensive review should evaluate tangible and intangible factors related to operations, industry dynamics, and organizational leadership.
2. Use insights gathered to establish next year's quarterly targets.
    1. Conduct preemptive risk analysis of potential issues based on established goals.
    2. Revise company values and operating agreements as needed to promote achievement.
3. Uplevel business strategy
    1. Consider whether the existing strategy disrupts the market and differentiates it from competitors. Assess the risk of being disrupted.

2. If you are the chief competitor, how would you undermine the current strategy?

One must carefully consider these questions to plan ahead, rather than reacting to unintended consequences in a post-mortem. This is especially prudent when the final outcome is consequential and irreversible.

When one comprehends the value proposition of a product, organization, or team, one becomes equipped to determine value-creation opportunities and build successful products accurately.

RECOMMENDED RESOURCE

Here are a few resources to help you create your own value proposition:

1. **Acquired Podcast:** An excellent podcast that does deep dives into the business models and strategy behind the most legendary companies and startups.
2. **Business Model Generation and the Strategyzer series:** An essential set of visual strategy tools and canvases for designing and iterating on innovative new business models.
3. **Competing Against Luck by Clayton Christensen:** The seminal book that introduced the "jobs-to-be-done" framework for understanding customer needs and focusing innovation efforts for maximum impact.
4. **First Round Review:** An incredible collection of tactical and actionable advice for entrepreneurs on hiring, management, and more from the perspectives of successful founders.
5. **Venture Deals and other books by Brad Feld:** Essential reading for gaining invaluable insights into venture capital, term sheets, valuation, negotiations, and more.
6. **The High Growth Handbook by Elad Gil:** A manual covering the most pressing challenge and opportunity when scaling a startup from the early stages up through IPO and beyond.
7. **BuiltIn city blogs:** Localized resources featuring local tech startups, city-specific job listings in major hubs,

and connecting founders to their startup communities.
8. **Lenny's Newsletter by Lenny Rachitsky:** A weekly publication read by tens of thousands offering tactical, no B.S. advice on launching and scaling breakthrough products.

I wish you the best in building products and services that truly resonate with your customers' jobs. If you would like to discover more business strategy or continue the discussion, follow me on LinkedIn (https://www.linkedin.com/in/deborahmillsscofield).

Made in United States
Orlando, FL
22 October 2025